# The Coach's Guide to Living Mindfully and Authentically

Galit Ventura-Rozen

Angela Giles

# COACH'S GUIDE TO LIVING MINDFULLY AND AUTHENTICALLY

## 22 Personal Stories of Self-Discovery and Fulfillment

**GALIT VENTURA-ROZEN & ANGELA GILES
WITH 22 AWE-INSPIRING WOMEN**

Copyright © 2024 by Everyday Woman, LLC

All rights reserved.

No part of this book may be reproduced in any form or by any electronic or mechanical means, including information storage and retrieval systems, without written permission from the author, except for the use of brief quotations in a book review.

The book compilation is initiated by Everyday Woman, LLC if you would like to be a published author etc etc visit www.everydaywoman.me/book or email us at everydaywomanco@gmail.com

Red Thread Publishing LLC. 2024

Paperback ISBN: 979-8-89294-000-9

Ebook ISBN: 979-8-89294-009-2

The information and advice contained in this book are based upon the research and the personal and professional experiences of the authors. Some names and characteristics have been changed, some events have been compressed, and some dialogue has been recreated. Chapters reflect the authors' present recollections of experiences over time. The opinions herein are of each individual contributor. All writings are the property of individual contributors.

The publisher and authors are not responsible for any adverse effects or consequences resulting from the use of any of the suggestions, preparations, or procedures discussed in this book.

# Contents

Introduction ............................................................. ix

**CHAPTER ONE** ............................................................. 1
*Focus on "The Thing"*
By Angela Giles

**CHAPTER TWO** ............................................................. 9
*Living with Internal Peace*
By Galit Ventura-Rozen

**CHAPTER THREE** ............................................................. 17
*The Mindful Coach*
By Coree Sullivan

**CHAPTER FOUR** ............................................................. 25
*Living with Grace: The Path to Mindfulness and True Self*
By Michelle Weihman

**CHAPTER FIVE** ............................................................. 33
*You Are Original: Brand Yourself!*
By Dr. Oyindamola Okenla

**CHAPTER SIX** ............................................................. 41
By Karen McDonald

**CHAPTER SEVEN** ............................................................. 49
*Resilience, Leadership, and Hope*
By Kathryn Whittington

**CHAPTER EIGHT** ............................................................. 57
*Talent Development: An Introspective Approach*
By Kelsey Paasch

**CHAPTER NINE** ............................................................. 65
*Dancing with My True Self*
By Maralana Shindelbower

**CHAPTER TEN** ............................................................. 73
*Living Authentically: A Transformative Guide*
By Melissa Trinci

**CHAPTER ELEVEN** — 81
*Ebracing Us: A Heart-to-Heart on Mental Fitness and Our Empowered Boundaries*
By Pearl Chiarenza

**CHAPTER TWELVE** — 89
*Beyond Instinct: Crafting Decisions with Mindful Intention*
By Rochelle Rondon

**CHAPTER THIRTEEN** — 99
*Embracing Authenticity in Social Media*
By Michelle Perkins

**CHAPTER FOURTEEN** — 107
*The Road to Wealth in a Weekend*
By Amanda Moxley

**CHAPTER FIFTEEN** — 117
*Look Inside Yourself, The Answer Is There*
By Nicole Toney

**CHAPTER SIXTEEN** — 127
*Yin and Yang, All at Once*
By Dr. Katy Chang

**CHAPTER SEVENTEEN** — 135
*Social Comparison ~ WE Will Not Conform to the "Norm"*
By Jennifer Kiser

**CHAPTER EIGHTEEN** — 145
*Success Redefined: Thriving Beyond Limits*
By Stephanie Freiboth

**CHAPTER NINETEEN** — 153
*Turning Soft Confidence Into Hard Evidence*
By Sami Lei

**CHAPTER TWENTY** — 161
*How To Outsmart the Distractions*
By Amy Elizabeth

**CHAPTER TWENTY-ONE** — 169
*My 9-Step Comprehensive Plan*
By Dr. Vicki D. Coleman

**CHAPTER TWENTY-TWO** — 183
*Coaches Empower Individuals to Maximize Their Potential*
By Nalo Thomas Mitchell

Thank You         189
Other Books       191

# Introduction

How amazing!!! This is our 6th anthology in three years. Over 200 women have now shared their stories with the world. Each woman has her own individual voice and journey. We at Everyday Woman are beyond thrilled to give all these women a platform on which to be authentic, genuine, and inspiring. These are everyday women just like me and you. Angela and I started this platform in one of the craziest times in the world: March 2020. We have helped thousands of women build their online branding and images through our TV network, www.everydaywomantv.com, where women can have their own TV show or watch other women share their expertise for free. As I mentioned, this is book number six, and there are many more to come. We have hosted Iconic Woman retreats, where women uplevel their branding through photo shoots, video shoots, training, and more. These are just a few of the wonderful things happening at Everyday Woman. Oh... and did I mention our Facebook group is almost 18,000 members?

With all this said, my point is this: if you think about it, you can create it and make it a reality. Ladies, it's your time. If you don't know where to start or how, reach out to us and let's talk. If you do know how...what are you waiting for?? everydaywomanco@gmail.com

My wish for you is that you stop waiting for the right time and stop using "I don't know how" as a reason not to try. If you fail, try again and again and again. You will get it right and you will succeed.

Xoxo
 Galit and Angela

www.everydaywoman.me
 www.everydaywoman.me/book

# Chapter One
## Focus on "The Thing"
## By Angela Giles

Angela Giles is a marketing pioneer, and she is a passionate communicator and mentor who is driven to help her clients become successful and effective in their fields. With nearly twenty years of experience in business and digital marketing, she has an innate skill of connecting with audiences of diverse backgrounds. She has helped over 2,000 business owners generate over $50 million in sales during the past twenty years. Her goal for each training is that each member of the audience leaves inspired, confident, and ready to implement change.

www.instagram.com/angelaksgiles/
www.facebook.com/AngelaKayGiles/
www.angelagiles.com

# Focus on "The Thing"

*By Angela Giles*

Welcome, daring trailblazers and aspiring empresses of the entrepreneurial jungle! You're about to embark on a transformative journey that challenges conventional wisdom and embraces a unique philosophy I call "simple secret, big results." Unlike the standard cheerleader, armed with fluffy words and feel-good mantras, I offer a different approach—straightforward, sassy, and no-nonsense. So, buckle up and get ready to dive into the world of focusing on "The Thing." "The Thing" will change your destiny.

## The Myth of the Superwoman: Debunking the Impossibility

The image of the superwoman is pervasive in our culture. She's the multi-tasking goddess, effortlessly juggling a myriad of tasks, always in control, never breaking a sweat. For real? What about behind the scenes when she breaks down and cries ugly tears? Or her personal life has gone to hell in a handbasket. Honestly, this image is not just unrealistic—it's harmful.

It sets an impossible standard that leads to burnout and disappointment. In reality, the pursuit of doing everything often results in achieving very little. All the projects you have started that you had great intentions for might not reach their peak if you are constantly trying to multi-task.

The toll of trying to be a multi-tasking superhero takes on mental and physical health is immense. It's time to shed this unrealistic expectation and embrace a more focused, sustainable approach.

## The Big Reveal: The Power of Singular Focus

Here's the heart of the matter: the key to exponential growth in your business isn't about *doing* more; it's about *focusing* more. To be precise, it's about focusing on one singular aspect: "The Thing." In a world that glorifies the hustle, this might seem counterintuitive. So many women define their success by all the tasks they have, and focusing on just one thing may be a hard pill to swallow. In fact, it could be a bitter pill to swallow. However, this singular focus is the gateway to phenomenal growth and unparalleled success in both your professional and personal life.

## Identifying "The Thing": Your Game Changer

Identifying "The Thing" is a critical first step. It's that pivotal aspect of your business that holds the potential to transform everything. This could range from your unique product to an innovative marketing strategy, from exceptional customer service to a groundbreaking business model. The challenge is to pinpoint that one element that, if elevated, could catalyze the most significant impact on your business.

To figure this out, the first thing you must do is figure out what you are most passionate about. Look at your current life and your business. What are things that you absolutely adore doing? Do those things bring you money when you do them? Are there people out there searching for the products or services that you offer? Doing the research and introspective into your soul will help you figure out what "The Thing" is for you!

## The Art of Obsession: Total Immersion in "The Thing"

Once "The Thing" is identified, it's time to become wholly obsessed with it. This obsession isn't about losing sight of everything else; it's about channeling your energies and focus into making "The Thing" the best it can be. It's thinking about it day and night, letting it permeate your dreams, and talking about it endlessly. This level of focus might seem extreme, but it's necessary for groundbreaking achievements. This is where you become your own biggest cheerleader.

## The Daily Ritual: Consistent Effort Towards Mastery

Incorporate "The Thing" into your daily routine. Make it a ritual. Whether it's fine-tuning a product feature, brainstorming marketing strategies, or enhancing customer interaction, every small effort counts. This consistent dedication is akin to muscle building—the more you work it, the stronger and more effective it becomes. Make sure that it is your number-one focus and it is non-negotiable to get that thing done or focused on. You deserve to focus on "The Thing" every day.

## Dealing with Distractions: Staying True to Your Focus

Distractions are inevitable. They appear as tempting new projects, enticing opportunities, or the latest social-media trends. The skill lies in recognizing these distractions and maintaining your focus on "The Thing." **Remember, every time you say "yes" to something not aligned with your primary goal, you're inadvertently saying "no" to potential growth in your business.** This is huge! It is a game changer when you can remember this. In fact, I would actually write this out and tape it to your mirror.

## The Domino Effect: Ripple of Improvements

Focusing on "The Thing" sets off a domino effect. Improvements in this one aspect begin to positively impact other areas of your business. For instance, enhancing customer service doesn't just satisfy customers; it leads to more referrals, better client retention, and an improved brand reputation. This ripple effect is a testament to the power of focused improvement. And that focused improvement will tend to spill over into your personal life.

## The Resilience Factor: Overcoming Challenges

Focusing on one thing doesn't guarantee a smooth journey. There will be obstacles, setbacks, and moments of doubt. Resilience is about staying the course, believing in your strategy, and persevering despite challenges. It's about being adaptable yet steadfast in your pursuit of excellence. And the thing about resilience is that as you grow in your efforts to focus on "The Thing," it will become easier over time.

## The Naysayers' Chorus: Staying Unwavering in Your Conviction

Be prepared to face skepticism and doubt. There will always be individuals who question your focused approach, advising you to diversify your efforts or chase the latest trends. While it's important to listen and consider different perspectives, ultimately, your commitment to your focused strategy must prevail. Personally, I never listen to negative Nellies. The way I see it is that everyone has an opinion, and your path doesn't need universal understanding; it requires your unwavering conviction.

## Learning from the Giants: Case Studies in Focus

Seek inspiration from successful entrepreneurs and leaders. In fact, make sure that your inner circle is filled with people who have forged the path before you. Study their journeys and you'll find a common theme: they didn't dilute their efforts. Instead, they identified their "Thing" and pursued it with relentless focus. Whether it's Steve Jobs's unwavering commitment to design aesthetics or Oprah's dedication to authentic storytelling, their success stories highlight the potency of concentrated effort. It really is a game changer!

## The Snarky Reality Check: Embracing Imperfections

Here's a candid truth: you're going to falter. There will be days when your focus wavers, you get sidetracked, or you start doubting your strategy. This is normal and part of the growth process. The key is to recognize these moments, learn from them, and realign yourself with your goal. Be sure to give yourself grace. Never beat yourself up. Instead, use the energy to re-focus.

## The Big Picture: Beyond Business Growth

The journey of focusing on "The Thing" transcends business growth. It's about personal evolution—becoming more disciplined, strategic, and aligned with your life goals. This journey is as much about crafting a successful business as it is about sculpting a formidable version of yourself. When I really got this concept, it began shifting my whole life. I became more focused on "The Thing" and less focused on stuff that really didn't matter. It has become so freeing.

## Conclusion: Embracing Your "Thing"

So, my fellow entrepreneurs, it's time to embrace your "Thing." Let go of the myth of the superwoman who does it all. Instead, channel your energies into this one transformative aspect of your business. Remember, the power of focus is not just in doing something well, but in doing the right thing exceptionally well.

Remember, this is **all** up to you. You are given the power to make choices every single day. You get to choose what "The Thing" is and whether you are going to focus on it that day or not. You are in charge of your destiny!

As you embark on this journey, keep in mind that it's not just about business growth; it's about personal mastery and creating a legacy that resonates with your deepest values and aspirations. So, rise up, focus, and let "The Thing" be the catalyst for your phenomenal success and fulfillment.

# Chapter Two
## Living with Internal Peace
## By Galit Ventura-Rozen

G alit started her entrepreneur career 25+ years ago in commercial real estate. She is Broker/Owner of Commercial Professionals in Las Vegas and has sold over $700 million in properties. She is co-founder of Everyday Woman TV, a 24/7 inspirational online network for women by women. She is a paid professional speaker and has spoken all over Canada and the United States on the topics of leadership, effective communication, mindset, and more.

Galit works with women privately to show them how to get to seven figures in their businesses by following the methods she has learned throughout her professional career, including those honed through owning and starting four businesses. She is the author of *The Successful Woman's Mindset,* her solo book, as well as six books she has put together with over 200 female authors.

Galit can be found on Linkedin, Tik Tok, Instagram, Facebook, and YouTube under Galit Ventura Rozen.

www.galitventurarozen.com

# Living with Internal Peace

By *Galit Ventura-Rozen*

In this fast-paced and demanding world we live in, finding internal peace has become a real mission for women everywhere. Think about it—we're constantly juggling personal and professional responsibilities, dealing with societal pressures, and sometimes it all gets overwhelming. But fear not! By understanding the importance of internal peace and implementing some kick-ass strategies, we can reclaim balance, harmony, and well-being in our lives and businesses.

    I am a woman who has worked since I was fifteen, had my first child at twenty-four, and four businesses by the time I was forty-five. Finding internal peace and nurturing it every day is a must in my life. I don't even know where my health or mindset would be if I didn't take care of myself daily. Often as women that becomes the last thing on our list every day. Even though it took me some time to recognize this, once I did it really was a game changer. I began setting up appointments with myself and waking up before everyone else so I had quiet time to put **me** 1st.

    What a foreign topic for so many of us and what a shame that it is. Why? Because how can we take care of everyone else if we are sick, don't have energy, are passing out at night, or just waiting to get into bed and starting the grind again every morning.

    Yes, it has taken time for me to master internal peace and, if I'm being completely honest, I still remind myself daily that without my internal peace, what is there? Worry, fear, constant anxiety? For me that was my reality for many years—going through life almost as if I was a robot checking off my daily to-do list.

    Do you know what internal peace is? It's that state of calmness, tranquility, and contentment that comes from deep within. It's not dependent on external circumstances; it's all about what's going on inside of us. So, how do we achieve this sweet state of mind? Well, it starts with some serious self-awareness, self-acceptance, and intentional practices. We must acknowledge and address the things that hold us back—self-doubt, negative self-talk, and the need for external validation. Trust me, I have experienced all these things over my lifetime—have you?

When we start down the road to internal peace.....

Oh, self-doubt...it can be a real buzzkill, can't it? But here's the deal—we can totally overcome it. It's time to kick that limiting mindset to the curb! Let's start by reflecting on ourselves and shifting those negative thoughts. We've got to challenge those beliefs and replace them with positive affirmations. Boost that confidence and embrace a more empowering mindset.

So, let's start by reflecting on ourselves and shifting those negative thoughts. Ask yourself, "What evidence do I have that supports these doubts?" Chances are, there isn't much. We often magnify our flaws and downplay our strengths, but it's time to challenge those beliefs. Take a moment to think about all the times you've overcome challenges, achieved success, or made a positive impact. You are a force to be reckoned with, my friend.

Now, let's replace those self-doubts with empowering affirmations. Remind yourself daily of your strengths, talents, and accomplishments. Repeat them like a mantra: "I am capable, I am worthy, and I have what it takes to succeed." Believe in yourself, because when you do, incredible things can happen.

Boost that confidence and embrace a more empowering mindset. Surround yourself with positive influences, whether it's supportive friends, mentors, or inspiring role models. Feed your mind with motivational books, podcasts that remind you of your limitless potential. And most importantly, be kind to yourself. Celebrate your successes, no matter how small, and remember that setbacks are just stepping stones towards growth.

You've got this, my friend. It's time to step into your power, banish self-doubt, and embrace the incredible person you are. The world is waiting for you to shine, so go out there and show them what you're capable of. Believe in yourself and the rest will follow.

Ladies, listen up! Self-care is an absolute must on our journey to internal peace. We often put others' needs before our own, leaving ourselves feeling drained and depleted. But hey, it's time to prioritize ourselves and show some love. Make self-care a non-negotiable part of your routine. Whether it's meditation, exercise, journaling, or indulging in your favorite hobbies—take that time for yourself each day. Trust me, it'll do wonders for your inner peace.

Alright, ladies, let's have a heart-to-heart about self-care. It's not just a luxury or an occasional treat—it's an absolute necessity on our journey to finding internal peace. We all tend to put others' needs before our own, leaving us feeling depleted and running on empty. But guess what? It's time to shift the focus back onto ourselves and show some much-needed love and care.

Now, I know what you might be thinking: "How can I possibly prioritize myself when there are so many demands and responsibilities?" Well, beautiful soul, it's time to make self-care a non-negotiable part of your daily routine. It's time to carve out that sacred space for yourself, where you can recharge, rejuvenate, and reconnect with your inner self.

So, what does self-care look like for you? It could be anything that brings you joy, peace, and relaxation. Maybe it's a morning meditation session to set the tone for the day ahead. Or perhaps it's lacing up your sneakers and going for a refreshing jog in nature. It could even be something as simple as indulging in your favorite hobbies, whether it's painting, gardening, or curling up with a good book. Whatever it is, make sure it speaks to your soul and fills you up from within.

Trust me when I say that incorporating self-care into your daily routine will do wonders for your inner peace. It's like giving yourself a warm hug, a gentle reminder that you deserve love and attention just as much as anyone else. By taking that time for yourself each day, you'll restore balance, replenish your energy, and cultivate a sense of well-being that radiates from within.

Remember, you cannot pour from an empty cup. Prioritizing self-care is not selfish; it's an act of self-love and self-preservation. By nourishing yourself, you become better equipped to show up fully for others, with a heart that is brimming with love and compassion.

So, let's make a pact, right here, right now. Promise me that you'll make self-care a top priority in your life. Promise me that you'll carve out that time for yourself, without guilt or hesitation. Promise me that you'll embrace the joy of self-care, savoring every moment of it.

You deserve this, my dear. You deserve to feel refreshed, rejuvenated, and at peace within yourself. Take that step towards nurturing your soul and watch as your inner peace blossoms into something truly beautiful. Your journey to internal peace starts with the simple act of prioritizing yourself.

Ever heard of mindfulness? It's a game-changer. Mindfulness is all about being present in the moment. No judgments, just paying attention to our thoughts, emotions, and sensations. Incorporating mindfulness practices—like meditation or simple mindful breathing exercises—into our daily routines can bring us relaxation, clarity, and inner calm. So, let's embrace the power of mindfulness and let our inner peace shine through.

You know what's awesome? Being true to ourselves! Society often puts pressure on us to conform or adopt different personas, but let's say no to that noise. True internal peace comes from embracing our authentic selves—living in alignment with our values, passions, and aspirations. When we're authentic, we experience freedom, fulfillment, and yes, that sweet inner peace.

Boundaries, they're everything. We need them in our personal and professional lives to stay sane and focused. It's time to set some healthy boundaries and protect our time, energy, and emotional well-being. Don't be afraid to say no to excessive demands. Prioritize what truly matters and create space for your inner peace to thrive. You deserve it!

Surround yourself with positive, uplifting people who have your back. Building supportive relationships is key for our well-being and inner peace. Seek mentors, join professional networks, or engage in communities that foster connection, collaboration, and empowerment. Together, we can create a supportive foundation for our personal and professional journeys.

Achieving internal peace is an ongoing journey. It's all about self-reflection, intentional practices, and committing to personal growth. We've covered it all: overcoming self-doubt, practicing self-care, cultivating mindfulness, embracing authenticity, setting boundaries, and nurturing supportive relationships. Remember, the power lies within you to unlock your own sense of peace. Get ready for a life filled with joy, purpose, and fulfillment. You got this!

# Chapter Three
## The Mindful Coach
## By Coree Sullivan

Coree Sullivan is originally from Northern Colorado and currently resides in Windsor, Colorado. She has two married daughters, six grandchildren, and four great-grandchildren. As a certified life coach, author, speaker and deep inner healing coach, Coree enjoys working with people to find the deep heart healing that helps them leave the pain of the past behind, so they can move forward into the life they were designed for.

As someone who's been through the painful journey of divorce, Coree studied to become a certified divorce recovery coach. She uses her training, as well as personal experience, to help others find their pathway to healing. In 2012 she authored the book *This Restored*

*Heart*, which is her personal testimony of healing and walking into a life full of the freedom and victory God designs for all of us to live. She has since gone on to author the best-selling book *Destiny After Divorce*. In this book she addresses the topics and material she utilizes for her successful divorce recovery classes and programs. You can find more information about her materials and programs at www.CoreeSullivan.com

# The Mindful Coach

*By Coree Sullivan*

As I sat in my cluttered office, surrounded by the chaos of deadlines and expectations, I couldn't shake the feeling that I had drifted away from my true self. The constant demands of my business had left me feeling disconnected and overwhelmed, yearning for a sense of purpose and authenticity.

Compounded by a recent divorce, these feelings also made me realize that I wasn't moving forward into healthy friendships or dating relationships. I had raised my girls as a single mom after their father and I divorced. My focus had become providing for them at that time, while trying to also chase things (including unhealthy relationships) to try and discover my authentic self. As a result, I finally realized I had lost me...a long time ago.

In my search for guidance, I attended group and private counseling sessions along with seminars on personal growth. I purchased several books and self-help programs as well. The truth is, however, I was not getting to the root of the real issues. I continued to feel triggered in some situations and be completely passive in others. My personal life was just as cluttered and chaotic as my office was.

Then I stumbled upon the concept of mindful coaching. I had heard about coaching but thought it was much like counseling. As I explored this new concept, I began to discover a beacon of hope, shining its light on a path for my transformative journey towards self-discovery and genuine connection to my authentic self.

Intrigued, but skeptical of the idea of reclaiming my true self, I decided to step into this journey, wanting to unravel the layers or pain and wounds that had kept me from living my true identity for so many years. Little did I know, this exploration would lead me down a path of profound awakening, where each mindful session became a sacred space for self-reflection and the discovery of my true self.

What is mindful coaching, you ask? It's a transformative approach of coaching that goes beyond conventional coaching methodologies, emphasizing on deep and intentional awareness of the present moment and how you got where you are. No cookie-cutter techniques here.

This coaching style provides space for the coach to guide the coachee to discover the root issues that have caused them to be trapped in old behaviors and triggers so that, through the process, they can become their authentic selves, discover their purpose in life, and live fulfilled lives. It helps pave the way for genuine connections, enabling the coaching process to unfold organically and authentically, ultimately leading to profound personal and professional growth.

When it comes to mindful coaching to discover authenticity, there are several general guidelines I've utilized that have proven to be helpful in achieving the coachee's goals. Keep in mind that these are not strict rules but rather principles to guide the coaching process.

Here are some of those guidelines.

**Create a Safe and Trusting Environment:**

Fostering a safe and non-judgmental space where the coachee feels comfortable sharing their thoughts and feelings is essential.

**Encourage Self-Reflection:**

Our stories have a lot to say about how we view our lives, which often dictates our values, beliefs, and experiences.

**Clarify Values and Priorities:**

Helping the coachee to identify their unique core values and priorities is key.

Guide them in aligning with these values can lead to a more authentic life.

**Mindfulness Practices:**

Introduce mindfulness techniques to help individuals stay

present and connected with their thoughts and emotions so they don't slip into old behaviors, triggers, and reactions.

**Challenge Limiting Beliefs:**

Identify and challenge any limiting beliefs that may be hindering authentic self-expression.

Encourage a growth mindset and exploration of new perspectives.

**Goal Setting:**

Collaboratively set goals that align with the coachee's authentic self.

Break down larger goals into smaller, manageable steps for sustained progress.

**Cultivate Self-Compassion:**

Help coachees understand that it's a process and it's important to be kind to yourself, non-judgmental, and compassionate during the journey of healing and self-discovery.

**Explore Life Narratives:**

Investigate personal narratives and stories that may shape one's self-perception and determine if they're based on true identity or are rooted in past wounds for self-protection.

Identify your unique, empowering narratives and challenge those that may be self-limiting.

**Celebrate Progress:**

Acknowledge and celebrate small victories and as you progress towards authenticity.

Reinforce positive changes to boost confidence and motivation.

**Feedback and Adjustments:**

Provide constructive feedback and support the coachee in making adjustments as needed.

Recognize that the journey towards authenticity is ongoing and may involve course corrections at times.

You are a unique individual! The coaching process is successful when it's tailored to your specific needs. Additionally, it's essential to be aware of and respect cultural and individual differences throughout the coaching journey.

Mindful coaching can have a transformative impact on various aspects of life. By incorporating mindfulness practices and coaching techniques, individuals often experience improved self-awareness, emotional regulation, and overall well-being. How would living your life authentically benefit you? Here's a glimpse into how life might look after engaging in mindful coaching.

**Increased Self-Awareness:**

Mindful coaching helps individuals become more attuned to their thoughts, emotions, and behaviors. After mindful coaching, many clients are more aware of their strengths, weaknesses, and patterns of behavior.

**Enhanced Emotional Regulation:**

Mindfulness techniques can empower individuals to manage stress and emotions effectively. Post-coaching, you might notice greater emotional resilience and the ability to navigate challenging situations with composure.

**Improved Relationships:**

Mindful coaching often addresses communication skills and empathy. As a result, your relationships with others may become more authentic, understanding, and fulfilling.

**Clarity of Goals:**

Through coaching, individuals often gain clarity on their values and aspirations. After mindful coaching, you may have a clearer vision of your goals and a roadmap to achieve them.

**Work-Life Balance:**

Mindfulness can bring a sense of balance between your work and personal life. You might find yourself better able to prioritize and allocate time to various aspects of your life.

**Mindful Decision-Making:**

Coaching encourages thoughtful decision-making. Following mindful coaching, you may approach decisions with greater awareness, considering the impact on your overall well-being.

**Enhanced Focus and Productivity:**
Mindful practices can sharpen focus and concentration. You may experience increased productivity and efficiency in both personal and professional endeavors.

**Resilience in Adversity:**
Mindful coaching often equips individuals with tools to navigate challenges and setbacks. After coaching, you might find yourself more resilient and able to bounce back from difficulties.

**Health and Well-being:**
Mindfulness is linked to better physical and mental health. Post-coaching, you may notice improvements in your overall well-being, including better sleep, reduced stress, and increased vitality.

**Lifelong Skills:**
Mindful coaching provides individuals with lifelong skills for continuous self-improvement. You may carry the benefits of mindfulness and coaching throughout your life, adapting them to evolving circumstances.

Remember that the impact of mindful coaching can vary from person to person. The journey is unique, and the outcomes depend on personal commitment and engagement with the coaching process.

I began my mindful coaching journey as a client over seventeen years ago. Once I experienced and completed my transformational journey, I wanted to help others who were struggling just as I had, I chose to enroll in a program to become a certified life coach who focuses on mindful coaching. I've been blessed to help many others find the freedom and authenticity I've found, so they, too, could become the best versions of themselves, just as I have. I find joy in helping others through mindful coaching.

If you find yourself amidst chaos, unfulfilled dreams, and a sense of living inauthentically, remember that the power to change lies within you. Embrace the journey of mindful coaching as a transformative path towards self-discovery and positive change. By cultivating self-awareness, setting meaningful goals, and fostering a deeper connection with your authentic self, you can navigate through challenges, unlock your true potential, and create a life that aligns with your values and aspirations. Your journey towards a more fulfilling and authentic life can begin with the conscious choice to embrace growth and embark on the path of mindful coaching.

> *"Authenticity is a collection of choices that we have to make every day. It's about the choice to show up and be real. The choice to be honest. The choice to let our true selves be seen."*
>
> — Brené Brown

Remember, living authentically is about embracing your uniqueness and being true to yourself in every aspect of your life. Indeed, it requires courage. It involves being true to yourself and embracing your values, beliefs, and identity, even in the face of societal expectations or judgment. Authentic living often involves self-discovery, self-acceptance, and the willingness to express your true thoughts and feelings. It can be a challenging journey, but many find it to be incredibly rewarding as it allows for a more genuine and fulfilling life.

# Chapter Four

## Living with Grace: The Path to Mindfulness and True Self

### By Michelle Weihman

Michelle Weihman, a celebrated nurse and empowerment coach with over 30 years of healthcare experience, has dedicated her life to nurturing and guiding others. Based in Las Vegas, she combines her extensive nursing wisdom with transformative life-coaching techniques, offering a unique approach to wellness and personal growth. Michelle is a passionate advocate for empowering women, drawing on her rich heritage from two strong grandmothers to inspire resilience and compassion in her clients. Her SELFCARE blueprint, deeply influenced by her familial legacy, underpins her successful practice. As the author of the bestselling book *Dare to Care* and host of the podcast *Dare to Care with Michelle*, she extends her message of holistic care and self-empowerment. Leading retreats and speaking events, Michelle's mission is to create a positive impact, emphasizing that caring—for oneself and others—is not just beneficial, it's cool.

www.linkedin.com/in/michelle-renee-weihman-bsn-rn-02a45196
www.instagram.com/michellereneeweihman/
www.facebook.com/profile.php?id=100067454403716v
www.michellereneeweihman.com/
www.tiktok.com/@daretocarewithmichelle

# Living with Grace: The Path to Mindfulness and True Self

By Michelle Weihman

**The Legacy of Lifetimes**

Our life's journey is similar to crafting a quilt, where each piece of fabric represents our experiences, values, and the wisdom handed down through generations. My own quilt is rich with the textures of care, resilience, and the enduring spirit of the incredible women who came before me: my grandmothers, Grace and Adeline. Great-grandma Grace was a centenarian who witnessed a world of change and kept her calm through quilting, and Grandma Adeline was a woman of unyielding spirit and energy, who embraced life with open arms, even doing something unexpected on her 80th birthday. Their stories and lessons are the vibrant patterns that color my approach to life and work, and they are perfectly aligned with my SELFCARE blueprint—a holistic approach that embodies Stillness, Energy, Love, Fearlessness, Compassion, Affirmations, Receiving, and Empowering. This blueprint guides my journey as a nurse, life coach, and empowerment guide, weaving together personal history and professional philosophy.

**Stillness: Grandma Grace's Quilt of Serenity**

Great-grandma Grace's moments of stillness were not solitary endeavors; they were also times of subtle teaching and sharing. I fondly recall how my young daughter would sit by her side, assisting in her own little way by picking up scraps of fabric. These were serene moments, filled with the quiet buzz of the sewing machine and the soft clatter of fabric pieces. For my daughter, Melissa, it was a game, but for Great-grandma Grace, it was a form of meditative practice—a way to instill the value of stillness in the bustling rhythm of life. This intergenerational bond, formed in the shared silence and simple tasks, taught us both the importance of finding peace in small, everyday activities. It is a lesson I carry forward: the art of weaving stillness into the fabric of our daily lives, creating pockets of calm and reflection amidst our ever-busy schedules.

**Energy: Adeline's Unyielding Spirit**

Grandma Adeline's energy was a testament to her unyielding spirit and her passion for life. This was nowhere more evident than in her remarkable decision to climb on my cousin's Harley Davidson motorcycle on her 80th birthday. It was a powerful display of her belief that age is just a number and that vitality springs from a zest for life. Her example taught me that true energy comes from an inner wellspring of enthusiasm and courage, and it is this lesson that I share in my work—encouraging others to embrace each day with vigor and joy, regardless of the challenges they face.

**Love: The Warmth of Adeline's Embrace**

Grandma Adeline's love was a palpable force, expressed through each meal prepared, every skinned knee bandaged, every tear wiped away with a comforting word. Her love was the strength that held the family together, an unspoken bond as nurturing and vital as a warm embrace on a chilly day. In my practice, I have learned to view love as the bedrock of healing. It is a journey that begins with self-love, creating a foundation strong enough to support others in their own paths to wellness and connection.

**Fearlessness: Embracing Change with Courage**

Fearlessness, as exemplified by my grandmothers, was not just about confronting physical challenges, but also about embracing the winds of change. Can you imagine the changes that my great-grandma Grace saw? Great-grandma Grace once told me the story of the first time she saw an airplane, a moment where awe mingled with fear, is a powerful testament to this. When she first witnessed that roaring machine flying above, she and her friend ran and climbed up on a fence, but when it flew over her head her instinctive reaction was to duck—an understandable response to the unknown. Yet, this story became a lesson in facing the new and the unfamiliar with curiosity rather than fear. It is a narrative I often reflect upon when encouraging others to embrace change. Fearlessness is about looking up, even when our instincts tell us to look down, and finding wonder in the unknown.

**Compassion: The Essence of Care**

Grandma Adeline's compassion was as tangible as the warm meals she lovingly prepared, not just for her family but for anyone who walked through her door. She believed that no visitor should leave her home hungry—be it for food, warmth, or kindness. This extended to all of God's creatures; even the family dog knew there was always a treat waiting. It was this all-encompassing compassion that has influenced my approach to care. Whether I am offering a listening ear or guiding someone through a difficult moment, I strive to pass on that same warmth and kindness, a tribute to the lessons of unconditional love and care I learned at her kitchen table.

**Affirmations: Grace's Melody**

Great-grandma Grace's resilience was anchored in her faith, reflected in the verses she read and the hymns she sang. These were not just words or melodies; they were her affirmations, her personal hymns of strength and hope. She used them to rise above life's challenges, anchoring herself in her beliefs. Inspired by her example, I have learned the power of affirmations in my own life and practice. Like Grace's hymns, they are tools for grounding, offering comfort and reinforcing our core values. In teaching others, I emphasize finding their own affirmations, their unique melodies of the soul, to navigate life's journey with resilience and positivity.

**Receive: The Art of Gracious Acceptance**

The art of receiving, a lesson subtly yet profoundly exemplified by my grandmothers, is about embracing life's offerings with openness and gratitude. It is about acknowledging that accepting help, love, or even a compliment is not a sign of weakness, but of strength. My grandmothers, in their unique ways, demonstrated this art. Whether it was Grandma Adeline welcoming a neighbor with a warm meal or Great-grandma Grace receiving a visitor's compliment on her quilting with a humble smile, they understood the power of gracious acceptance.

In my journey as a nurse and a life coach, I have come to realize the significance of this lesson. Receiving is as much a part of the give-and-take of life as offering is. It allows us to experience the full spectrum of human connection, from giving support to accepting it. It is in this exchange that relationships are strengthened, and communities are built. I encourage others to open their hearts to receive, not just material things, but the intangible gifts of life: love, support, wisdom, and even challenges that foster growth.

**Empower: The Chapters of Legacy**

The principles of empowerment that Great-grandma Grace instilled in our family found their way into the pages of *Dare to Care*, a testament to the legacy she left behind. It was almost serendipitous how the chapters my cousin Billie Jo and I wrote independently mirrored each other in values and insights. This similarity is a powerful reminder of the deep-seated empowerment that runs through our veins—a force that compels us to uplift, to guide, and to inspire courage in others just as it was once instilled in us. *Dare to*

*Care* is more than a title; it is a call to action that encapsulates the essence of our shared journey and the strength we offer to those we serve.

**Crafting a Legacy of Love and Empowerment**

In the intricate quilt of our lives, every patch represents a moment, a lesson, or a memory. The rich stories of my grandmothers, Grace and Adeline, have been essential pieces in my quilt, imbuing it with strength, wisdom, and compassion. These lessons have not only shaped my personal journey but also deeply influenced my approach as a nurse and a life coach. Their teachings about stillness, energy, love, fearlessness, compassion, and the power of affirmations are woven into my SELFCARE blueprint, guiding my practice and philosophy.

Our life's quilt is more than a collection of individual experiences; it is a legacy we create and share. As you add to your own quilt, consider the values and lessons that each piece represents. Let this quilt be a reflection of your journey, your growth, and the impact you have on those around you. In nurturing ourselves and extending care to others, we stitch together a life of richness, purpose, and connection.

And in all that you do, always remember that caring is cool.

# Chapter Five
## You Are Original: Brand Yourself!
### By Dr. Oyindamola Okenla

Dr. Oyindamola Okenla is an award-winning and best-selling author and a JM-certified coach, speaker, and trainer. With her extensive leadership experience spanning over two decades, she founded Hilltop Transformation Academy, LLC, where she directs the transformative Fresh Start Meadows program. Dr. Okenla, who holds a doctorate in pastoral psychology and a board-certified master's in mental health coaching, brings extensive and profound expertise.

Her signature program, EmpowerHER, emphasizes authenticity and purpose, especially in the aftermath of toxic relationships. A staunch advocate for personal branding, Dr. Okenla believes in its power to establish a genuine and resilient presence, particularly for those reclaiming their intrinsic worth after trauma. For deeper insight into her work, especially on overcoming toxic relationship challenges and the importance of personal branding, visit her website.

www.instagram.com/coachdto/
www.facebook.com/CoachDTO/
www.damolatreasureokenla.com/
www.tiktok.com/@coachdto

# You Are Original: Brand Yourself!

*By Dr. Oyindamola Okenla*

On the joyous occasion of my niece Busayo's high-school graduation, the faculty representative's words echoed in my heart, "**How can we forget the brand, Busayo?**" This simple yet profound statement rekindled a deep conviction within me about the power of authenticity. Busayo had etched a memorable mark, not by being a mere replica of others, but by staying true to her essence.

Over the years, in my journey as a coach, I have emphasized repeatedly to my clients, friends, and acquaintances the importance of living one's original self. To attempt to embody another person's life or ideals can lead to a life that is complex, clumsy, and confusing. Such a way of living can result in individuals feeling lost, adrift in a sea of societal expectations, and disconnected from their core.

The Bible, in its infinite wisdom, encapsulates this sentiment beautifully in Psalms 139:14-16: "I thank you, God, for making me so mysteriously complex! Everything you do is marvelously breathtaking."

The challenge people face today is the societal pressure to fit into pre-defined molds, to adhere to certain expectations, and to live a life that may not resonate with their true selves. Such pressures often stem from not recognizing one's worth and value.

> To be yourself in a world that is constantly trying to make you something else is the greatest accomplishment.
>
> — Ralph Waldo Emerson

Dr. Brené Brown, a renowned research professor, mentions in her studies on vulnerability and courage, "Authenticity is a collection of choices that we have to make every day. It is about the choice to show up and be real. The choice to be honest. The choice to let our true selves be seen."

One of the most profound challenges people face in living authentically is the inability to recognize and embrace their inherent worth. This lack of self-worth often stems from several factors including the following:

## 1. Societal Expectations and Comparisons:

We live in a world that incessantly compares. From material possessions to job titles, from physical appearances to social-media likes, comparisons are rampant. This continuous juxtaposition often makes individuals feel less than if they do not "measure up."

Over time, people may internalize these comparisons, leading to feelings of inadequacy. This can inhibit them from expressing their true selves, for fear of not being "enough."

## 2. Past Failures and Criticisms:

Past experiences, especially those steeped in failures, criticisms, or rejections, can deeply shape how one perceives oneself-worth. When not processed healthily, these events can inflict lingering emotional scars. It becomes all too easy for individuals to start interpreting these events as the sum of their identity. Bound by these past narratives, they may find themselves trapped, unable to embrace authenticity in the present moment. I, too, once found myself ensnared in such a predicament. Due to an incident, people began questioning my credibility and my authority to guide others, particularly because of my marital status. This skepticism seeped into my psyche, and for a while, I lost my confidence. However, with introspection and a rediscovery of my purpose, I began to reaffirm my identity and my commitment to my vocation.

### 3. Perceived Lack of Achievements:

We tend to view success in terms of achievement. If individuals feel they have not achieved "enough" by a certain age or stage in life, it can lead to feelings of diminished self-worth. This can stifle their willingness to take risks, explore new avenues, or express their genuine thoughts and feelings. They might conform to others' expectations, thinking it is the "safe" and "accepted" route.

### 4. Lack of Self-awareness:

As mentioned earlier, self-awareness is the compass of authentic living. Without it, individuals might remain oblivious to their strengths, passions, and values. Not recognizing one's strengths can result in a life lived on others' terms. Without clarity on what they stand for, individuals can easily drift, adopting personas that aren't genuinely theirs.

### Key Points:

1. **Self-awareness is Paramount:**

Delve deep within yourself. It's essential to unearth the core of your being and to recognize and appreciate your strengths, vulnerabilities, and uniqueness. Regular introspection, journaling, and seeking feedback are instrumental in this journey. I always tell myself, "**I am a treasure, not trash!**"

2. **Value & Self-worth:**

Recognize your intrinsic value. Many fall into the trap of societal expectations because they don't appreciate their worth. Positive affirmations, surrounding oneself with uplifting individuals, and challenging negative self-beliefs are vital. Who are the people you surround yourself with? Are they encouragers or discouragers?

3. **Intentionality & Consistency:**
Life requires purpose and consistency. Setting clear goals, visualizing them, and consistently checking in on one's actions ensures alignment with the authentic self.

4. **Embrace Vulnerability:**
True strength lies in accepting one's vulnerabilities. Engaging in profound conversations, expressing fears and dreams, and accepting imperfections are all part of this process.

5. **Personal Branding:**
Just as a brand has a unique identity, so do you. Audit your online and offline presence, ensuring they align with your true self. Engage authentically, form connections based on genuine interests, and project an authentic image.

**Action Points:**

- Engage in self-reflective practices like journaling and meditation.
- Establish clear boundaries against societal pressures and negative influences.
- Continuously educate yourself, challenging societal narratives and norms.
- Prioritize mental well-being, seeking professional help if required.
- Engage in activities that foster creativity and self-expression.

Living authentically is not just about being true to yourself; it's about understanding your unique value and then projecting that value to the world. This is where the essence of personal branding intersects with authentic living. There are benefits of connecting to your authentic self. Ten of those benefits are listed below.

1. **Inner Peace and Brand Consistency:** When you live authentically, your brand naturally remains consistent. This internal alignment translates into a coherent and trustworthy image for the outside world.

2. **Improved Relationships and Network Growth:** A genuine personal brand fosters trust. The deeper and more meaningful relationships that come from authenticity can expand your network and opportunities.

3. **Enhanced Decision-Making in Brand Choices:** Knowing your true self allows for clear decisions about what aligns with your brand and what does not, ensuring every choice strengthens your brand identity.

4. **Greater Self-Confidence and Brand Presence:** Embracing your true self boosts your confidence, making you more assertive in promoting your brand and standing out in a crowd.

5. **Increased Resilience in Brand Challenges:** Authentic brands, built on real values and experiences, are more resilient to criticism and challenges, allowing them to endure and evolve.

6. **Authentic Growth and Brand Evolution:** As you grow and evolve authentically, so does your brand, ensuring it remains relevant and relatable.

7. **Enhanced Creativity and Brand Innovation:** Authenticity frees up mental space, driving innovation and keeping your brand fresh and dynamic.

8. **Better Physical and Mental Health, and Brand Longevity:** An authentic brand is sustainable. It is not a facade you put on, but rather an extension of your true self, ensuring longevity and reducing the stress of maintaining a false image.

9. **Personal Integrity and Brand Trustworthiness:**

Your brand's credibility is rooted in your integrity. An authentic life ensures that your brand remains trustworthy and respected.

10. **Fulfillment and Brand Satisfaction:** A brand built on authentic living ensures not just success, but also fulfillment. It means your brand is not just known, but also loved and celebrated.

In the vast market of personal brands, authenticity is the distinguishing factor. It is what sets you apart, resonates with others, and gives your brand its unique flavor. As highlighted within this book, recognizing one's true value and forging an authentic path are not just beneficial for personal well-being, but also crucial for building a strong, recognizable, and trustworthy personal brand. This practice is a declaration to the world: "I am original. This is my brand."

Remember, the world does not need a replica; it needs the original you. In my years of counseling and coaching, this has been my most vital lesson: stay genuine, and brand yourself with authenticity. As you journey through life, strive to be the best version of yourself, the original you, and watch as the world recognizes and remembers your unique brand. Embrace yourself, for you are original. Embrace your brand, for it is like no other.

In a world awash with facades, what truly resonates is authenticity, not perfection. People are yearning for genuineness amid the overwhelming sea of pretense. So, rather than concealing, wear your insecurities with pride and recognize your inadequacies. Yet, always remember to elevate those qualities that set you apart. You have been meticulously crafted by a divine hand, singular in design and purpose. Revel in the unmatched brilliance of your authentic self. **Be you. Freely. Joyfully!**

# Chapter Six
## By Karen McDonald

Karen McDonald is CEO, founder and visionary of Wise Owl Legal Practice Management Software for law firms. She has been involved in law-firm accounting software support for over 25 years. This certainly has earned her the title of "The Wise Owl"!

Karen has an accounting degree and a passion for best use of technology. She is forever figuring out how to use technology to improve efficiency and productivity and has many tales to tell. Like many of us, she has been through the pain of a divorce and survived, becoming stronger and wiser! She has worked in the world of accounting and accounting software, including roles in accounting firms, government and industry.

Her favorite business books are *7 Habits of Highly Effective People* and *The Ultimate Sales Machine*.

Karen lives in Brisbane, Queensland, Australia with her husband, Bill. Away from the computer she loves Smokey, her Maltese Shih Tzu, waterfalls, and the great outdoors.

www.instagram.com/wiseowllegal/
www.facebook.com/wiseowllegal/
www.wiseowllegal.com.au/

# When Life Gives You Lemons, How Do You Make Lemonade?

*By Karen McDonald*

### *Introduction*

Pondering on my being so incredibly "self sufficient" undoubtedly links back to the life-changing event that happened when I was five years old.

I have mentored many people along my journey. Seeing people achieve their dreams is one of the things that truly brings me joy. It is so incredibly exciting to listen to someone talk about a pipe dream and quiz them more about it and helping them brainstorm a vision of how to bring it to life.

Watching people who have achieved their goals also brings me joy, and I love to learn from them.

Having mentors in our lives is of great benefit to accelerate our journey; however, we can also accelerate our journey by mentoring ourselves as well. An everyday woman can move into greatness far more easily when it is a natural flow.

In high school I was a lost soul. I had fabulous grades but felt lost amongst the hugeness and business of the world. I was certainly not in the "hip" crowd.

Even in those formative years I was very self-sufficient. Six months of weekly Friday-afternoon sewing classes in year eight and I was off and running! Once I got my hands on a sewing machine, I took hold of those weekly classes and taught myself to make some amazing tailored creations.

I looked to many sources of strength and inspiration in the first few years out of school. Over time, and many life experiences, I came to learn that I could determine my own destiny.

What is living mindfully and authentically? To me, it is acting from a pure heart with honest intentions. Living mindfully and attentively allows life to flow so much more smoothly!

## **The Story of Self-Discovery**

I still remember the 2:00 a.m. banging on the front door by the police with the awful news that my dad had been killed in a tragic road accident.

From a very young age, I went out with my dad, a carpenter, a lot on the weekends. My grandmother would tell me I could name all his tools. Mum had another two children and then when I was five years and seven months old, my dad was killed instantly in a car accident.

My mum had been a naive, shy, country girl who had followed her man to Sydney to grow his career. Suddenly he was gone and Mum was left with three children aged five, two, and a baby who had turned one year old only fifteen days before.

To make things more complex the house Mum and Dad had bought was part-way through a massive renovation. Once the relatives went home, I suddenly was the next in line, and I had to grow up instantly.

I had just started school in Sydney. Mum sold the house, returning to Brisbane and family support.

After Dad's death, Mum was in a massive turmoil, as to be expected, and cried every night for two years.

Two or three years after Dad's death, Mum took a full-time job with a law firm in the city of Brisbane CBD. My grandma and her sister, my aunty Julie, took turns, week about to mind us after school. I worked hard right through primary and high school; my world was more responsible and more serious than my classmates.

The first year out of school my fascination with computers started. I rearranged my part-time accounting course to start the computing subjects early. Programming in COBOL on punch cards began a lifelong fascination with computers.

After marrying and having two children, I moved to New

Zealand, the homeland of my first husband. We lived there for two years with two young children, with the expectation of staying permanently.

Amidst homesickness and an unfinished Australian accounting degree, not expecting to return to Australia to live or work, I filled up my university electives with computer subjects. That move was gold!

Two years later, in 1994, I returned to Australia, finally having finished my degree, as a single parent needing to start again! I soon landed a job at Griffith University in Brisbane as a finance coordinator for the Library and Information Technology departments, a job I held for four years.

As a single parent, my children and I were a close-knit team. There was Saturday sport and lots of school commitments. I tried to get out in the bush as often as possible. We did a lot of camping and took an extra day off every long weekend to extend our getaways. When there wasn't a camping trip, I tried to get in an outdoor walk in as often as possible. I found I could sneak in a two-hour *bush* walk at Cedar Creek Falls on a Saturday or Sunday afternoon, even if life was busy.

During the 1990s I read every self-help and personal-development book I could get my hands on. It all started with *The 7 Habits of Highly Effective People*, by Stephen Covey.

When people operate from centers like money, visibility, position, status and so on, it is obvious and people feel insincerity. When a person operates from a principle-centered position, others can feel that position. It breeds trust.

*The 7 Habits of Highly Effective People* continues to be a milestone in my life to this day. I have given copies of the book to several people, not always to see it returned! Curiously, I have been the recipient of several free copies of *7 Habits*. Each time, receiving this precious gift has made me feel that the universe has my back.

I came to realize I didn't need to subscribe to every concept in all of the books I would pick up, but if I could find two or three gems from a book I was way ahead.

In more recent times, I have begun to follow Simon Sinek, who talks about finding your why and how working from that place allows motivation to flow naturally.

Whilst working at Griffith University, I did a one-day speed-reading course—that, too, was life-changing. I probably initially underestimated the impact of that course. I have since suggested many colleagues hunt down a good speed-reading course.

In 1997, a year after leaving Griffith University, I started Cascade Accounting Solutions, helping small-business owners computerize and automate their administrative overhead. This business has morphed into a full-service accounting firm and last year, 2023, Cascade celebrated 25 years!

### *Key Principles and Practice*

Mindset is everything! I have always had a lot going on and I know to keep up the pace I set for myself, it is really important to have good sleep. I don't know how to "do nothing" and have no desire to learn!

There are many times people can rest on their laurels and wallow in "poor me." My mum "got on with it" after my dad died, and personally, from age five, I didn't know any other way.

Finding our happy place/s helps a lot. For me, that is on a mountain top or at a waterfall.

I am pleased I do have a switch where I can focus on things and get lost in what is in front of me—be it a waterfall, a mountain top, a task at work, or a sewing project. Sometimes when I have had really tragic things happening in the background, I have been able to flick that switch and escape the other reality in my life for a while and achieve some big things. That doesn't mean I don't grieve or process the bad things.

Guard your sleep. Sleep is incredibly important and valuable. Do not ever cheat on sleep. You will definitely lose!

If something is interrupting my sleep, it is a red flag for me that something needs to be fixed and **now**!

Since January 2016, I have used an app called The Daily Calm. There are two features of this app that are beneficial to me: the first is a ten-minute meditation, which I do each day. The second feature (and probably the best benefit of Daily Calm) is the sleep stories. If my mind is running at 100 miles an hour, instead of sleeping, I put on a sleep story. They are wonderful. They grab my attention enough to stop me from trying to solve the problems of the world, but not enough to keep me awake.

As of today, I have used the Daily Calm app 270 days straight! My prior record was 268 days.

### *Conclusion*

We have one life; every day is a choice. It is our choice day by day to choose to be victorious or to be a victim. Living mindfully and authentically empowers us to choose the victorious route, and this path is far more fulfilling and satisfying.

Mindset is everything! Very few people don't go through hardship and pain of some sort. How we deal with it and move on makes the difference.

We only live once! So, make it count!

What are your motivators? I encourage you to take time to find out what motivates you and to find out what your happy place is. Both of those are foundational rocks when the storms come.

What inspires you to crash through barriers, glass ceilings, or the many stumbling blocks life throws at us?

Every day is a choice! When life gives you lemons, how do **you** make lemonade?

# Chapter Seven
## Resilience, Leadership, and Hope
### By Kathryn Whittington

Kathryn Whittington was elected to serve on the Ashtabula County Board of Commissioners on January 3, 2017, for a four-year term of office. Commissioner Whittington was re-elected to serve an additional four-year term of office to begin on January 3, 2021.

Since elected, Kathryn has been working diligently on the drug epidemic locally, statewide and nationally. She has created an initiative, Rural America, and spoken across the country on the prevention efforts and successes of Ashtabula County. Kathryn supports law enforcement and was instrumental in the creation of the new Crime Enforcement Agency of Ashtabula County (CEAAC), a drug task force that serves Ashtabula County.

Kathryn was previously employed with Ashtabula County Children Services, serving the children and families of Ashtabula County for 15 years, and she has over 25 years of experience working with families and communities. She was formerly the community service coordinator for Ashtabula County Children Services Board and served as the interim chair of the OneOhio Foundation Board.

Kathryn currently serves as the chair for the Health & Human Services Committee through the County Commissioners Association of Ohio, as the sub-committee vice-chair for the Human Services and Education Steering Committee through the National Associations of Counties, and as chair of the One Ohio Foundation Board.

Kathryn is a West Geauga High School graduate, has an Associate's Degree in Business Administration Management and a Bachelor's Degree in General Business Administration.

www.linkedin.com/in/kathryn-whittington-21804a42/
www.instagram.com/vote_kathryn_whittington
www.facebook.com/kathryn.whittington.75?mibextid=LQQJ4d

# Resilience, Leadership, and Hope

By *Kathryn Whittington*

In the tapestry of life, some threads are woven with challenges, adversities, and unexpected turns. I never aspired to be a writer; my dream was simpler yet profound—to serve others. Today, I share my story not as a tale of victimhood but as a testament to resilience, leadership, and unwavering hope. This narrative is not just mine; it's a beacon for those who may feel alone, a source of inspiration for realizing lifelong dreams, and a call to make a difference in our communities.

My journey is intertwined with my faith, identity as a Christian, a wife, a mom, a nana, a public servant, a speaker, a presenter, and an advocate for children and families. My faith has been a constant staple in my life when other things were not. I knew very young that I was called upon to serve others. Serving was something that came very easily for me. I worked hard to make sure that I served others in a manner that God sent me here to do. When it came time for a career, social services chose me. Yes, that is correct: it chose me. My degrees are actually in Business Administration, Management, and Finance. The positions I applied for were always focused on children and families in need. So, I embarked on a social-service career that has spanned over 25 years and has been driven by my faith and love for Christ.

Raised in the Methodist faith, my spiritual foundation became my rock when the world seemed uncertain. My faith journey has been a steadfast anchor in the tumultuous sea of life's uncertainties. It is a source of strength that has been pivotal in overcoming adversities and celebrating triumphs. In these pages, I share not just my story but also the profound role that faith has played in my life and the successes it has ushered in.

Motherhood, with its blessings and heartbreaks, has been a central theme in my life. As a mom and stepmom to five children, the challenges of raising a family became even more pronounced when addiction cast its shadow. Raising three granddaughters, a responsibility thrust upon me by unforeseen circumstances, has become a reminder of the profound impact addiction can have on both the individual and the entire family. The harsh reality of the national drug epidemic hit home in 2013 when my house was burglarized. It was a night that marked not just the loss of material possessions but also a profound awakening to the harsh realities of addiction. The intrusion, born out of desperation, left me grappling with the aftermath and fueled a personal commitment to addressing addiction in our community and nationwide.

Having witnessed firsthand the destructive force of addiction, my life took on a new purpose. The burglary, a pivotal moment in my life, propelled me further into the realm of advocacy. Determined to be a voice for those affected by addiction, I embarked on a journey as a speaker and presenter at various drug epidemic forums. My presentation, "Rural America: Tackling the Drug Epidemic," born out of my experiences, underscores the power of partnerships and local efforts in combating the pervasive drug epidemic afflicting communities nationwide. It seeks to shed light on the impact of addiction and emphasizes the role of partnerships and local efforts in combating this pervasive issue. It is my hope that sharing my story ignites a spark in others to join the fight against addiction.

Driven by a deep-seated desire to witness positive change and growth in my home county, I made the bold decision to run for the office of Ashtabula County Commissioner. When my journey began, I knew that my faith would carry me through no matter what happened. What I was not prepared for was that during my campaign my faith would be questioned and challenged by others. I had never encountered this before. I found myself wanting to take and protect what I believed in.

It was clear to me that our collective voice was not resonating as it should. Once elected, I realized that being actively engaged in my community was not enough; I needed to extend my reach to the state and federal levels. Eager to establish myself and make a meaningful impact, I grappled with the nuances of leadership. The challenges of being a female elected official were stark, requiring me to establish myself, earn respect, and hone my leadership skills. Recognizing my need for growth, I sought guidance and mentorship from fellow women leaders, participated in leadership programs, and emerged ready to chart a new course in my political leadership to navigate the complexities of my position.

The intimate encounter with addiction within my family sparked a personal mission to support others facing this insidious disease. As a speaker and presenter at various drug-epidemic forums, I passionately share my story, emphasizing the crucial role of partnerships and local efforts in combating the drug epidemic. Through my presentation, "Rural America: Tackling the Drug Epidemic," I seek to inspire others to get involved, foster hope and resilience in the face of adversity, and to let people know they are not alone.

Having spent time at Children's Services, I had already established connections with many local liaisons. Building on these relationships, I began to expand my network. Elevating my advocacy, I became actively involved at the state and federal levels through committees at the County Commissioners Association of Ohio and the National Association of Counties. I understood that building partnerships is not confined to the local arena; it extends to statewide and national levels. The impact of such collaborations can be directly felt at the grassroots level. This is how active involvement and cultivated relationships at the state and national levels have directly influenced positive change in Ashtabula County.

My commitment to human services, children services, and criminal-justice advocacy led to significant contributions at both the local and state levels. In the realm of advocacy, being appointed to boards is not just beneficial; it's essential. It ensures that our county has a seat at the table and a voice that demands to be heard. As I navigate challenges unique to Ashtabula County, I draw upon my abilities to bring people together for the greater good and extend my leadership skills beyond the confines of traditional governances, reflecting a commitment to the holistic well-being of my community.

Becoming an elected official allows me to tell the story from a different perspective than most. I have met individuals who do not know how they will get through the day—let alone where the next meal, shelter, clothing, and basic hygiene items will come from. I have volunteered my time throughout my lifetime to allow my hands to be the physical tools, doing God's work through me.

This journey of advocacy, partnership building, and legislative involvement serves as a testament to the transformative power of my commitment to my community. By actively participating in state and national dialogues, Ashtabula County has seen tangible improvements, and this is only the beginning. As a woman dedicated to positive change, I am fueled by the belief that collective action can reshape the narrative and elevate the lives of those we serve.

I have time and time again been afforded the opportunities to take an idea and bring community stakeholders to the table, and we leave that table with a plan to execute serving our communities and their needs.

For me, success is the positive difference my actions and decisions make in Ashtabula County. As the largest county geographically in Ohio, our challenges were met with collaborative efforts. I spearheaded the creation of a dedicated drug task force, reflecting my commitment to fostering community growth and resilience.

The tapestry of my story is woven from the threads of my life's experiences. More than a memoir, it is a beacon of hope for those navigating their own trials and tribulations. It is my wish that, by sharing my story, readers will find solace, clarity, and inspiration.

From the ashes of personal adversity rose a woman of strength, resilience, and leadership. As I share my journey, I wish to inspire others to find hope in the darkest moments, to realize that they are never alone, and to recognize the power each of us holds to make a difference. This is a testament to the enduring truth that no one walks alone. I am Kathryn Whittington, Ashtabula County Commissioner, and this is my story—a testament to the transformative power of faith, service, and leadership.

# Chapter Eight
## Talent Development: An Introspective Approach
### By Kelsey Paasch

Through a tailored coaching program and personalized mentorship, Kelsey offers small business owners invaluable insights, guidance, and strategies to navigate the complex landscape of leadership. Whether it's developing short and long-term business goals, implementing effective execution strategies, optimizing operational processes, or developing cohesive team cultures, Kelsey is committed to equipping leaders with the tools they need to succeed. With a customized and personal approach, Kelsey understands that each leader faces unique challenges and takes a holistic approach, considering the individual's aspirations, strengths, and areas for growth. By fostering an environment of trust and collaboration, Kelsey helps leaders gain clarity, develop resilience, and build the confidence necessary to overcome obstacles and achieve their goals.

With her guidance, support, and unwavering belief in your potential, you can confidently navigate the challenges of leadership and build a thriving business that reflects your unique vision and values.

The time is now! Invest in you. Invest in your business. Invest in your future.

www.linkedin.com/in/kelseypaasch
www.instagram.com/kelsey_e_paasch/
www.facebook.com/Kelsey.E.Paasch
www.contourconsulting.co

# Talent Development: An Introspective Approach

*By Kelsey Paasch*

In the ever-evolving landscape of the professional world, organizations are constantly seeking to optimize their talent pool for sustained success. However, when faced with challenges in talent performance, it is not merely enough to address surface-level issues; a more profound understanding of the root causes is essential. By acknowledging and dissecting the underlying factors contributing to talent issues, leaders not only pave the way for effective solutions but also foster a culture of continuous improvement within their organizations. This exploration underscores the importance of introspection and strategic self-assessment as indispensable tools for leaders navigating the complexities of talent management.

I was recently coaching a client who was frustrated with the talent of a key leader within their organization. My client shared his pent-up frustration with one of his key leaders failing to deliver on what my client perceived were essential tasks of the leader's role. After listening to my client share specific examples of these key "failures," I asked him how long these concerns had been there, and he shared that it had been happening for over a year. I then posed this question to him: "Are the issues a result of the employee's lack of performance, or a lack of performance by you?" After a brief pause, he said "Tell me more."

As a business coach, I work every day with leaders who face challenges in navigating the world of talent management. Whether in a small business, a large company, or a not-for-profit organization, leaders face similar challenges in hiring, onboarding, and retaining employees who possess the quality of talent necessary to deliver expected results. When leaders see an employee struggling to perform effectively in their roles, it can be easy for a leader to assume that the employee is not right for their organization and that the employee must go. However, leveraging years of experience in talent management, I challenge my clients to think beyond the surface performance issues and identify the root causes of the employee's deficient performance. In doing this, my clients can address the root issues, allowing leaders the opportunity to course correct the performance concerns. If business leaders learn to identify where performance gaps are, it allows them to help correct the behavior instead of it requiring turnover. To help my clients identify these root causes within their organizations, I introduce them to three critical questions that every leader needs to ask themselves when assessing talent-performance issues.

The first question is, "**Have I set clear expectations?**" Clear expectations can be provided to employees in a variety of ways including job descriptions, individual quarterly plans, and/or directional or strategic company plans. Does your team have current, accurate job descriptions? Have you supported them in creating the quarterly plans necessary to deliver on the company's yearly directional plan? This first focus acts as a guiding beacon for both leaders and team members, highlighting what is expected of both the organization and the employee. Ambiguity in expectations leads to confusion, resulting in misdirected efforts and unmet goals. Effective leaders take ownership of this by ensuring that all team members comprehends their roles and how they will deliver their work to align with the company objectives.

The second question to ask is, "**Have I provided all the necessary tools and resources to allow them to effectively do their job?**" Empowering individuals with the necessary resources enables employees to execute tasks with efficiency. Imagine asking a deep-sea diver to explore the dark waters without an oxygen tank. It sounds extreme, but how often do leaders set an expectation while not understanding or listening to employees when they tell leadership what is needed to effectively execute the task they have been given? As leaders, it is important to not only understand the tangible tools needed but to also include training, mentorship, and access to information when assessing the support needed by employees. It is also essential that leaders regularly engage their teams to understand what tools or resources the individuals perceive as necessary to effectively perform their tasks as opposed to leadership assuming they know what tools are needed. By actively engaging with their teams and reacting to the necessary needs, leaders signal their commitment to nurturing growth and facilitating success within their teams.

The third question to ask is, "**Have I provided regular and consistent feedback?**" It is common for people to associate feedback with a negative and uncomfortable connotation, causing this leadership tactic to be one of the hardest to consistently execute as a leader. However, if done properly, feedback should follow a simple formula: seek to understand the current state of the situation, reinforce the expectations, and ask what support the individual needs in meeting the expectations. By utilizing this format, leaders engage their employees to understand what is going on, revisit the expectations, and put the individual in control of what they perceive as necessary to do their job. Regular feedback acts as a compass, steering employees toward improvement and growth. It is not a mere formality but rather a catalyst for progress. Effective leaders foster an environment where feedback flows freely, fostering continuous learning and development.

So how did my client assess himself after considering these three questions? After thoughtful discussion, my client was able to identify that the performance concerns did not lie solely with the individual. There were gaps in expectations as there was no clear job description for this employee, and no company directional plan had been shared with the team or this individual. Additionally, any feedback that had been shared was not provided in a consistent and timely manner, leaving the employee unaware of the depth of performance concerns my client had. Once my client understood these two areas of opportunity, he took accountability and worked closely with the individual to address these two areas. Weekly one-to-one meetings were scheduled with recurring calendar invites, allowing for weekly alignment on performance and work objectives between my client and the employee. A current job description was created and shared with the individual, and a yearly directional plan was shared so that the employee could create their quarterly documents in alignment with the organizational plan. The individual engaged with my client, and together they worked to help close the performance gaps that had been identified. This example is a great success story of supporting a current employee within a role, versus the costly impact of having turnover in a key leadership position. Subsequently, retaining this employee resulted in other team members engaging more effectively with this key leader, allowing my client to focus on other key areas of the business. This example highlights that while talent development can be challenging, utilizing these three simple questions can help create an amazing success story.

Conversely, if a leader can confidently adhere to all three pillars and yet an employee continues to underperform, the issue may indeed lie with the employee. In these instances, it becomes incumbent upon the employee to evaluate their commitment, capability, and contribution to the team. If no such ability is possible with the employee, the leader must act quickly to remove the individual before their lack of performance begins to impact team culture, customer service, and/or company performance.

Now the question is, how can you as a leader apply this strategy to the leadership of your own team? Just as I challenged my client, it is important for you as a leader to assess whether you have upheld the three pillars of effective talent management. Have clear expectations been set? Have the necessary tools and resources been identified and provided? Has feedback been consistently shared? If you as a leader find yourself unable to answer in the affirmative to these questions, you must acknowledge that the issue may not solely rest with the employee, but there may be opportunities for growth within your own personal leadership approach. A lack of clarity, inadequate resources, or inconsistent feedback could be contributing factors to an employee's underperformance. In such cases, you as a leader must be introspective, recalibrate your approach, and address these deficiencies to set the stage for success.

As you reflect on this innovative approach, I encourage you to think of how the integration of simplification and intentionality in talent development can not only propel individuals toward exceeding performance expectations, but also simultaneously also lay the foundation for a dynamic and thriving organizational culture. By fostering engagement, motivation, and a commitment to excellence, this approach positions organizations to not only retain and nurture existing talent but also to attract new, high-caliber individuals. As business leaders navigate the ever-evolving landscape of professional development, the commitment to a simplified and intentional approach becomes the compass guiding us toward sustained organizational success and individual growth.

# Chapter Nine
## Dancing with My True Self
## By Maralana Shindelbower

Maralana Go Do Be, an author and empowerment coach with over a decade of experience, is a beacon of authenticity and confidence. With boundless energy and a multifaceted personality, Maralana is dedicated to guiding women through life transitions, inspiring them to lead authentically awesome lives.

In her upcoming book, Maralana shares insights into multifaceted life-building, blending personal anecdotes with actionable steps. Her quirkiness shines through as she imparts valuable lessons, making her book a refreshing and relatable read.

Beyond writing, Maralana impacts lives through group programs, coaching, and dynamic speaking engagements. The creator of journals, workbooks, and the host of *Big Girl Adventure Life*, she breaks barriers and encourages plus-size women to embrace outdoor adventures.

Maralana's journey is a movement toward empowerment, authenticity, and realness, offering readers an inspiring and uplifting path to transform their lives authentically. Get ready to embark on a journey of empowerment, confidence, and boundless possibilities!

www.Instagram.com/maralanaGoDoBe

www.Facebook.com/MaralanaGoDoBe

www.Maralana.com

# Dancing with My True Self

*By Maralana Shindelbower*

Let me take you on a little journey, one that's all about finding your authentic self. It's like putting on your favorite lipstick and realizing, "Yes, this is me, and I'm ready to strut my stuff!" So, grab your comfy chair, a cup of tea, or a glass of wine—let's chat about embracing and being our fabulous, authentic selves.

I have to confess: it wasn't too long ago that I found myself living in a world where authenticity was like a rare gem—hard to come by. The pressure to fit in, to conform, to be what everyone expected me to be was real. I'd catch myself wearing masks more often than accessories. But that was then. Today, I want to share my own journey to authenticity with a dash of humor and a sprinkle of sass, just like me.

Picture this: I used to feel like a chameleon in a world full of flamingos. I'd change colors to blend in, hoping I'd finally fit the mold and belong. But let me tell you, it was exhausting. Pretending to be someone I wasn't was like wearing heels on a hiking trip, which can be done, but let's be honest: it would be uncomfortable and blister-inducing. What I learned, though, is that every facet of my life has its place and they don't have to commingle.

*Tip: Identify a situation where you've felt the need to blend in and reflect on how it made you feel. Acknowledge the discomfort and imagine shedding that chameleon skin.*

**Mindfulness: My First Step to Freedom**

The turning point in my journey to authenticity was the day I discovered mindfulness. It's like slipping into a cozy pair of slippers after a long day in stilettos—a relief and sanctuary. Mindfulness allowed me to slow down, breathe, and really notice what was going on inside and around me. Suddenly, I could hear my own voice, which had been whispering my truth all along without the expectations or "shoulds" involved.

I used many tools to practice mindfulness and dig deep: it's just a matter of how to make it work for you. The key is to start, jump in, dabble, and see what works for you.

**Start the Day with Intention:**

Kick off each day with some intention-setting. It's not just a morning routine; it's a mental huddle, getting those positive vibes going for the day ahead. Think about your own mantra or intention that vibes with your goals, setting the stage for a focused mindset.

**Cultivate Meditation:**

Add a bit of meditation to your daily routine, treating it like a mental gym to flex that self-awareness and focus. Find a meditation technique that clicks with you, whether it's a guided app, transcendental meditation, or good old mindfulness. The trick is to make it a habit, something that nurtures mental clarity and resilience.

**Just Breathe:**

In the craziness of modern life, we often forget the magic of just breathing. But in those stress-packed moments, it's a game changer. Try a simple breathing exercise like the "4-5-6" technique: inhale for four, hold for five, exhale for six. It's your portable Zen zone for regaining composure amidst life's chaos.

**Engage Your Senses:**

Life often rushes by, and we forget to savor the richness of our surroundings. Engaging your senses is like pressing pause and really tuning in. Taste your food, feel the sun on your skin—be present in the moment. It's a practice that transforms ordinary experiences into extraordinary moments.

**Slow Down:**

In a world that's always rushing, slowing down becomes a rebellious act. I encourage you to savor the process, appreciate the details, and find joy in the journey. It's not about how fast you reach the destination, but rather relishing every step along the way.

**Limit Distractions:**

Screens, notifications, constant connectivity—they all vie for our attention. Consider reducing screen time, putting away your phone, and creating tech-free zones. Trust me, it's a remarkable factor in fostering a more mindful and present life.

By slowing down and being mindful I've discovered that all the facets of my life are important to make me whole, not just the ones that I'm a master at or make money on. I can be the woman who dances like no one's watching (even when people are watching), the weekend warrior doing a rain or snow dance in the outdoors, and the mom hosting toddler dance parties. Pursuing all of what makes my heart skip a beat has been therapeutic, and mindfulness opened up my eyes to accepting all these facets of myself. Besides, life's too short for beige when you're meant to shine in technicolor.

*Tip: Identify one passion you've neglected. Schedule dedicated time for it this week. Observe how it infuses your life with vibrancy.*

## **The Power of Unapologetic Authenticity**

The cherry on top of this fabulous journey: embracing unapologetic authenticity. Now, I walk into a room and own it like a queen strutting down a runway. I've learned that the world doesn't need another copy; it needs the mosaic masterpiece that is me—and the masterpiece that is you.

And again, it's putting in the work to find the swatches that make up you.

### Fostering Self-Reflection:

Let's kick off the authenticity journey with a bit of self-reflection. Try a weekly journaling gig, your own little space where you reflect on moments that felt true and those times you felt a bit disconnected. This reflection gig becomes your compass, pointing you toward choices that sync up with your real self.

### Establish Boundaries:

In the era of constant hustle, clear boundaries are like gold. Whether it's carving out a physical space, declaring a "tech-free" hour, or saying "no" to extra commitments, make a boundary plan that's all you. It's your shield, keeping that authenticity intact in the middle of life's chaos.

**Embrace Vulnerability:**

Authentic living loves to dance with vulnerability. Challenge yourself to open up, share a real emotion or a personal story with someone you trust. This vulnerability exercise isn't just about baring your soul, it's about building deeper connections and setting the stage for authentic relationships.

**Honest Communication:**

Authentic connections thrive on honest conversations. I've embraced expressing my thoughts and feelings sincerely. It's liberating and lays the foundation for genuine connections. No masks, no costumes, just me.

**Pursue Your Passions:**

Authentic living is my ode to joy. I dedicate time to activities and hobbies that light up my soul. Life's too short to settle for anything less than what genuinely makes me happy.

**Self-acceptance:**

Lastly, I've learned to be my own biggest fan. Imperfections are the brushstrokes of my uniqueness. Self-acceptance is a daily practice of kindness towards myself.

Remember, these aren't rules; they're companions on a journey. Mindfulness and authenticity are ongoing dances. I often find solace in journaling and sometimes lean on the wisdom of other coaches and support groups. It's my way of nurturing these qualities in my daily life.

*Exercise: Embrace one aspect of yourself that you've been hesitant to share openly. It could be a talent, a quirk, or a belief. Revel in the liberating feeling of unapologetic authenticity.*

Alongside these, here's a personal challenge: pick one thing from the mindful approach and one from authentic living to weave into your daily routine for the next two weeks. Take a moment to reflect on the experience—notice how it tweaks your mindset, your emotions, and your connections.

By weaving these practices into your daily life, you're not just tinkering. You're diving into a personal evolution journey. These mindful and authentic-living practices aren't just about getting through the day; they're about crafting a life where intention shapes your mornings, meditation anchors your days, mindful breathing keeps you grounded, self-reflection lights your path, boundaries preserve your authenticity, and vulnerability becomes the source of genuine connections.

This chapter is not just me dancing my dance—it's about giving you the tools to create your own dance that's authentically yours. Let this journey guide you toward a life where every intentional step, every mindful breath, and every vulnerable moment brings you closer to your most authentic self.

So, my friends, let's make a pact: let's all raise that glass (or teacup) to living mindfully authentic, embracing our quirks, and letting our true selves shine. Life is too short to be anyone but the incredible, authentic you. Cheers to dancing through life in our own fabulous style!

# Chapter Ten

## Living Authentically: A Transformative Guide

### By Melissa Trinci

Melissa Trinci is a dynamic transformational coach and accomplished entrepreneur, dedicated to guiding individuals to unlock their innate potential. As a reiki master teacher and neurolinguistic programming master, she skillfully blends various holistic practices to facilitate profound personal growth and healing. With a track record of building several successful mid-six-figure businesses from the ground up, Melissa brings a wealth of practical, real-world experience to her coaching, helping clients navigate complex personal and professional landscapes.

Her approach is deeply empathetic and strategically focused, emphasizing the breaking of generational cycles and fostering a mindset of abundance and well-being. Melissa provides a sanctuary for transformation, offering tailored tools and insights to shift clients from merely surviving to thriving. Committed to empowering her clients, she creates personalized pathways to success, ensuring each individual is equipped to live a fulfilling, purpose-driven life. With her guidance, clients learn to tap into their own wisdom, activating the changes necessary for a prosperous and harmonious life.

www.instagram.com/melissatrinci/
www.facebook.com/mtrinci
www.melissatrinci.com
www.tiktok.com/@melissatrinci
www.twitter.com/melissatrinci

# Living Authentically: A Transformative Guide

*By Melissa* Trinci

Hi there! I'm Melissa, your guide on this transformative journey toward self-discovery. Join me as we explore the twists, turns, and lessons that have shaped my pursuit of fulfillment, with the hope of inspiring and empowering you on your own path.

In my years of serving both myself and my clients, a common thread emerges: a yearning for external forces to catalyze meaningful change. Often, we seek a magic wand to dispel the barriers that hinder our progress. However, the truth is that the power to transform resides within each of us, ready to be harnessed.

Unlocking the incredible potential within our minds is a transformative journey. As we learn to access and harness this latent power, we open doors to astonishing capabilities and boundless creativity. The intricate workings of our minds, once understood and utilized, enable us to navigate challenges with newfound resilience. Embracing this journey not only enriches our personal growth but also unveils the profound impact our minds can have on shaping a fulfilling and purposeful life.

## The Core of Authentic Living

The foundation of mindful and authentic living lies in a profound understanding of ourselves. My personal journey spans decades, marked by a relentless pursuit of healing modalities to overcome trauma, physical ailments, and finding the strength to lead a healthy and authentic life. Certified in energetics, neuro linguistic programming, and the trauma healing method, my Quantum Shift Program stands out as the linchpin in my transformative toolkit.

Following the steps in this program resolved my "fibromyalgia," eased my anxiety, and allowed me to grow multiple businesses with confidence and in a state of ease and flow. My personal and professional relationships improved substantially. I have a peace, joy, and understanding that I never thought possible.

When you take your power back and unlock your true authenticity, nothing can stop you.

**Quantum Shift Program Insights:**

- **Understanding the Brain:** Unraveling the mysteries of the subconscious mind, understanding its information processing, and delving into the influences that shape our perception of safety can offer life-changing revelations.
- **Subconscious Beliefs:** Recognizing limiting beliefs that no longer serve us and understanding their conflict with our conscious desires empowers us to rewire these beliefs and reshape our reality.
- **Emotional Mastery:** Attaining mastery over our emotions involves accessing, understanding, processing, and releasing them in a healthy manner, recognizing their role in serving us.

**Knowledge is Power**

Knowledge is the key to power, especially when it comes to understanding our patterns, cycles, and minds. These insights and techniques empower us to cultivate the life we've always dreamed of, fostering personal and professional growth with reduced anxiety and struggle.

Implementing these tools in my life deepened the impact of other healing modalities. The process of achieving personal and professional goals became smoother, with less anxiety and struggle. I stepped into authenticity without feeling like an imposter, leaving self-sabotage in the past. I was able to watch my dream life come to fruition, and this made me want to continue to dream bigger and continue the process!

When you have the power to understand yourself, everything is possible. When you access and change the beliefs that no longer serve you, you change your life.

## A Lifelong Journey

Unlocking the incredible potential within our minds is a transformative journey. As we learn to access and harness this latent power, we open doors to astonishing capabilities and boundless creativity. The intricate workings of our minds, once understood and utilized, enable us to navigate challenges with newfound resilience. Embracing this journey not only enriches our personal growth but also unveils the profound impact our minds can have on shaping a fulfilling and purposeful life. This transformation is not fleeting; it's a lasting imprint that stays with us throughout our life's journey.

This is something that stays with you for the rest of your life. As we continue to dream bigger, delve deeper into self-discovery, and create new horizons in both our personal and professional lives, we inevitably encounter a multitude of beliefs and challenges. The encouraging news is that, armed with the ability to harness our inner power, it becomes progressively easier to recognize the recurring cycles and initiate the necessary changes. With each challenge faced, the honed skill of navigating these intricate mental landscapes becomes a testament to the enduring strength derived from understanding and utilizing the incredible power within. The journey is an ongoing exploration marked by continuous growth, resilience, and a deepening connection with the profound capabilities residing within the realms of our own minds.

**The World Needs You**

I truly believe that each and every one of us has gifts that the world needs. We are unique humans who have a specific calling in our lives, and that is what you are feeling when you desire more, when you are dreaming about all the possibilities, and when you feel compelled to do the things that are constantly on your mind.

We all have a circle of influence and a responsibility to heed the call to be our beautiful, authentic selves to serve ourselves, our families, friends, and the world. When we are unable to move in that authenticity, when we are unable to move forward and instead continue to self-sabotage, we are not filling that calling in our lives. The world needs you.

The fact that you are reading this book speaks to the fact that you are seeking a deeper, more fulfilling life. That you are ready and willing to live in a mindful and authentic way. That you have dreams for your life that are just waiting to be created. That you have something inside of you that the world needs. I encourage you to keep going, keep seeking, and keep doing the work needed to come into alignment with those dreams.


**Practical Tips for Getting Started:**
    **Write out your dream life.**

No holding back. Dream big!

Be specific! You want to really get into the details of what your day-to-day life looks like from the moment you wake up to the moment you go to sleep.

What is your morning routine? How do you feel? Where do you live? What is your family life like? Who are you serving? Where do you vacation? Don't hold back for the sake of being practical. Dream big!

**Identify doubts and fears to recognize existing belief systems.**

Now it's time to write down all the doubts and fears that came up for you while you were writing out your dream life. These are your subconscious beliefs that are causing the struggle you feel when trying to create this life. These are your limiting beliefs.

**Counter disbelief by listing what is true and the beliefs you want to instill.**

Now to take all those limiting beliefs and fears and counter them! What do you know to be true? What do you want to believe instead? It's time to create the story you want to be true to you.

Now that you have an idea of the limiting beliefs, you can begin to understand the misalignment between your subconscious and conscious mind. Now, you can begin to see where the struggle and frustration come from.

**An Invitation to Expand**

If you are ready to expand on your understanding of where these beliefs originated, follow these journaling prompts as well:

**Explore Beliefs' Origins:**

- Journal about family and early influences.
- Uncover intentionally and unintentionally passed-down beliefs.
- Understand cultural influences shaping your aspirations.

**Role of the Observer:**

- Become an observer in your life and journal what you see.
- Clearly see patterns and cycles to initiate lasting changes.

If you find yourself resonating with these words, know that there is much more to explore. I yearn to share additional insights about these processes and hope that we can connect in diverse ways. As you embark on the journey of trusting and believing in yourself, rest assured that I am cheering you on.

Embrace your unique journey with an open heart and mind. Authenticity, not perfection, is the goal. Let your inner light guide you, secure in the knowledge that you are precisely where you need to be.

May your journey be marked by curiosity, empowerment, and a revitalized commitment to living mindfully and authentically. Your story is yours alone—share it, live it, and love it. And as you continue this enriching exploration, remember: I'm here with you every step of the way, championing your unique and magnificent journey.

# Chapter Eleven

## Ebracing Us: A Heart to Heart on Mental Fitness and Our Empowered Boundaries
### By Pearl Chiarenza

A mental-fitness life coach, author, and captivating speaker, Pearl champions women's journeys to self-discovery and unapologetic self-care.

Leading you on a transformative path where mind, body, and spirit unite, crafting your narrative as your own SHERO (Strong, Happy, Empowered, Radiant, Original) is her mission.

Offering one-on-one and group coaching, Pearl's expertise

extends to vibrant community SHERO gatherings and empowering women's pajama retreats of self-renewal. With unwavering zeal, she equips you with the superpower of a positive mindset, helping you triumph over life's trials with a cape of resilience.

Pearl's expertise is underscored by certification as a mental-fitness trainer and a literary portfolio, including *Behind Her Brand* and *Women's Guide to The Mindset of a Successful Woman*.

Pearl's featured in various magazines; an honorary day in Syracuse, NY; and the prestigious Women of Worth Award. She is a mom to two adult sons and a loving wife to Chuck, her husband of 37 years.

www.linkedin.com/in/pearl-chiarenza-8269a8b/
www.instagram.com/pearl_chiarenza/
www.facebook.com/pearlchiarenza
www.wsliving.com/
https://www.tiktok.com/@pearlchiarenza

# Ebracing Us: A Heart to Heart on Mental Fitness and Our Empowered Boundaries

*By Pearl Chiarenza*

Hey love, there's something I want to share with you—this journey into mental fitness and setting boundaries. Life can be a wild ride, right? So, let's dive into this chapter where we uncover the secrets to living authentically and embracing our own power. This isn't just a chat about theories; it's a guide for you, for us. Come along as we explore why this matters, what's in it for you, and how we can light up our lives.

## Understanding the Concept of Living Mindfully and Authentically:

Alright, imagine our minds getting a spa day. That's what living mindfully is all about—dealing with work stuff, family drama, or whatever with a zen-like calmness. And authenticity? It's about being unapologetically us, quirks and all. Picture our everyday adventures getting a serious upgrade. Let's talk about how these things can make our world even more awesome.

## Key Principles and Practices:

Now, let's get down to the real talk—the good stuff we can actually do. Self-compassion is like being your own best friend. Radical acceptance is making peace with the messy, imperfect parts of us. Boundaries? They're like our superheroes—we'll chat not just about why they're crucial but also how to set them, so our well-being takes center stage. And intentional living? It's about making choices that truly reflect who we are. Let's make these principles our own, babe.

   **1. Self-Compassion:** At the core of authenticity is kindness towards oneself. Self-compassion involves recognizing and embracing our imperfections. We all have quirks, make mistakes, and go through challenging moments. It's accepting that this is part of the shared human experience. Instead of being our own harshest critic, let's be comforting friends to ourselves, acknowledging that, hey, it's okay not to be perfect.

**2. Radical Acceptance:** Authentic living involves acknowledging and embracing the reality of the present. It allows you to make peace with imperfections, creating space for growth and self-discovery. Acceptance starts with acknowledging and understanding reality as it is, without adding layers of judgment or resistance. It's facing the truth head-on, even when it's uncomfortable, without getting entangled in a web of "shoulds" or "could haves."

**3. Boundary Setting:** Boundaries are the unsung heroes of mental fitness. Before setting boundaries, it's essential to understand your own needs, values, and priorities. Reflect on what truly matters to you and what contributes to your well-being. This self-awareness forms the foundation for creating boundaries that align with your authentic self. The magic word is "no." Learning to say "no" is not a rejection of others; it's a prioritization of yourself. Saying "no" when needed is an essential skill for preserving your energy and preventing burnout.

**4. Intentional Living:** Every choice we make shapes our journey. Intentional living is about aligning your actions with your values, creating a life that reflects your true essence. It starts with a deep understanding of your core values. What truly matters to you? What do you prioritize in your life? **Clarifying your values provides a compass for making intentional choices.** Rather than pursuing goals for the sake of external validation, intentional living involves setting goals that resonate with your values. These goals become milestones on your journey, guiding you towards a life of purpose and fulfillment.

# Common Obstacles and Strategies for Overcoming Them

In pursuit of mindful and authentic living, you may encounter obstacles: societal expectations, self-doubt, or the sheer busyness of life.

**Societal Expectations:** Societal norms and expectations can often pressure individuals to conform to predefined roles and behaviors, hindering authentic expression. By establishing a strong sense of self-awareness, you can recognize when external expectations clash with your authentic self, and consciously choose authenticity. Surround yourself with a supportive community that values individuality.

**Self-Doubt:** Inner critics and self-doubt can cast shadows on the path to authenticity, making individuals question their worthiness. When we cultivate self-compassion, we acknowledge and challenge negative self-talk. Celebrate your strengths and achievements. Seek support from friends, mentors, or therapists to gain perspective and build confidence.

**Time Constraints:** Busy schedules and numerous responsibilities can make it challenging to find time for mindfulness practices and self-reflection. It is important that we prioritize self-care and mindfulness. Start with small, manageable practices, like brief moments of deep breathing or mindfulness exercises. Create dedicated time slots for self-reflection, even if they are brief, to foster a sense of mindfulness within your daily routine.

**Fear of Judgment:** The fear of being judged or criticized can deter individuals from expressing their authentic selves. Practicing self-acceptance and acknowledging that not everyone will understand or appreciate your authentic choices allows you to focus on building a supportive network that values your uniqueness. As confidence grows, the fear of judgment tends to diminish.

**Comparison Trap:** Constantly comparing oneself to others can lead to feelings of inadequacy and a skewed sense of authenticity. Shifting your focus inward allowing yourself to regularly reflect on your values, strengths, and goals creates a practice of gratitude for your unique journey. You should also limit your exposure to social media if it contributes to unhealthy comparisons and, instead, embrace the beauty of your individual path.

**Overcoming Past Trauma:** Past traumas can cast long shadows, making it challenging to fully embrace the present and live authentically. Seeking professional support to process and heal from past traumas allows us to learn to practice self-compassion, understanding that healing is a journey. Allow yourself to engage in mindfulness practices to stay present and cultivate resilience.

**Resistance to Change:** Embracing authenticity often involves change, which can be met with resistance. Taking gradual and mindful steps toward authenticity can ease the discomfort of change. Break down larger goals into smaller, manageable tasks. Celebrate each small victory, reinforcing the positive aspects of the change process.

**Perfectionism:** The pursuit of perfection can hinder authentic expression, as individuals fear showing imperfections. Challenging the notion of perfection and embracing the beauty in imperfections allows us to see them as opportunities for growth. Set realistic expectations, understanding that authenticity often involves vulnerability and learning from mistakes.

Remember, the journey toward mindful and authentic living is unique to everyone. It's okay to face obstacles, and it's okay to seek support. By acknowledging challenges and actively working to overcome them, individuals can foster a more resilient and empowered approach to living authentically.

In concluding this heart-to-heart, let's cherish the idea that living authentically isn't a final destination, but rather an ongoing journey. Consider these principles not as abstract ideas but as tangible tools in our relationship toolbox, designed to enhance our connection and individual well-being.

Your call-to-action is an invitation to weave these insights into the fabric of your life. Take these bits and pieces, make them uniquely yours, and embark on a journey where authenticity becomes your superpower. Picture yourself navigating life armed with the strength of your genuine self. It's not just a philosophy; it's a commitment to shaping a life that feels genuinely and wonderfully yours. Are you ready to embrace this adventure?

# Chapter Twelve
## Beyond Instinct: Crafting Decisions with Mindful Intention
### By Rochelle Rondon

R ochelle Rondon, a marketing executive, bestselling author, business consultant, and coach, with over two decades of pioneering strategies that lead businesses to unparalleled success. Her career, spanning arts, community events, and work with World Vision Canada, has come full circle as she has returned to her hometown of Mississauga, drawn by its vibrant culture.

Rochelle's visionary approach and deep understanding of consumer behavior, market trends, and cutting-edge technologies enable her to craft tailored marketing solutions for clients. Her ability to blend innovation with proven methodologies empowers businesses to seize new opportunities and dominate their industries.

Throughout her illustrious career, Rochelle has held senior roles at notable organizations like MySayToday, Chestnut Park Real Estate Limited, Fusion, and Operation Smile. Her achievements have earned recognition from the Canadian Marketing Association and the Data & Marketing Association for her data-driven and innovative strategies.

www.linkedin.com/in/rochellerondon1/
www.instagram.com/rochelle_rondon_/
www.rondonway.ca

# Beyond Instinct: Crafting Decisions with Mindful Intention

*By Rochelle Rondon*

Life is a dance, a journey that calls us to chase change and success. Yet, halfway through, we may find ourselves daydreaming about whether we've truly crafted the life we long for or fallen prey to survival instincts over intentional decision-making. This reflection is not about right or wrong paths, but rather acknowledging the potential for better choices beyond basic survival instincts.

In my 30s, I vividly recall aspiring to the perfect nine-to-five job, envisioning myself as a mom, and dreaming of owning a thriving business by the age of 40—a millionaire's dream, indeed. While these aspirations were commendable, the reality that unfolded was not without its share of challenges. Achieving those dreams demanded relentless effort and unwavering support. It became clear that what sets individuals apart is not merely the goals they set, but also the drive and intention fueling their journeys.

For women embracing empowerment, a pivotal moment arrives when they must explore the possibilities of mindful decision-making, transcending instincts and tapping into a profound sense of knowing. This involves cultivating a gut feeling and life grit that propel them toward a life of clarity, reducing reactive responses, and ushering in less stress with decisions that yield better results.

As we embark on this transformative journey, let's open our minds into an expanded exploration of empowering tips:

**Cultivating Self-Compassion:**

In the heart of mindful decision-making, self-compassion plays a pivotal role. Acknowledge that, as human beings, we are fallible. Mistakes and setbacks are not failures, but rather opportunities for learning and growth. Approach yourself with kindness, understanding that the path to intentional living is a continuous evolution.

Embracing self-compassion is not a sign of weakness, but rather a testament to your humanity. Reflect on the challenges you've faced and recognize them as stepping stones toward personal growth. This compassionate perspective allows you to navigate decisions with a sense of resilience, fostering a mindset that embraces the ebb and flow of life's complexities.

**Nurture Positive Relationships:**

Decisions are not made in isolation; they ripple through the fabric of our relationships. Foster connections that align with your values, as they contribute to a supportive environment for mindful decision-making. Surround yourself with individuals who inspire and challenge you, enhancing the quality of your choices.

Building and sustaining positive relationships requires conscious effort. Engage in open communication, actively listen to others, and cultivate empathy. In the realm of decision-making, collaborative insights from trusted confidantes can provide valuable perspectives, enriching the tapestry of your choices.

**Integrate Mindful Decision-Making in Daily Rituals:**

Extend the principles of mindful decision-making into your daily rituals. From morning routines to evening reflections, infuse intentionality into every action. This practice not only reinforces your commitment, but also establishes a harmonious rhythm in your life.

Consider incorporating mindfulness practices, such as meditation or mindful breathing, into your daily routine. These rituals serve as anchors, grounding you in the present moment and fostering a heightened awareness that extends into your decision-making processes.

**The Power of Visualization:**

Envisioning your goals with vivid detail enhances the potency of mindful decision-making. Picture the outcomes you desire, creating a mental roadmap that guides your choices. Visualization serves as a powerful tool, aligning your subconscious mind with your conscious intentions.

Take time to visualize not only the end result, but also the journey itself. See the challenges as opportunities for growth and visualize the steps you'll take to overcome them. This proactive mental imagery instills confidence and resilience, empowering you to navigate decision crossroads with clarity.

**Seek Continuous Learning:**

Embrace a mindset of continuous learning. Curiosity fuels mindful decision-making, prompting you to explore new perspectives and ideas. Attend workshops, read diverse literature, and engage in conversations that broaden your understanding of the world, enriching the palette from which you draw your decisions.

In the pursuit of continuous learning, consider exploring topics beyond your immediate expertise. Exposure to diverse fields and ideas cultivates a broad perspective, enabling you to approach decisions with a nuanced understanding. Embrace the intellectual curiosity that propels you toward informed and intentional choices.

**Establish Boundaries:**

Mindful decision-making involves knowing when to say "yes" and when to say "no." Establish clear boundaries that safeguard your well-being and align with your priorities. Recognize that setting boundaries is an act of self-respect, contributing to a balanced and intentional life.

Boundary-setting requires a deep understanding of your values and priorities. Reflect on what truly matters to you and consider how each decision aligns with these fundamental aspects of your life. Boundaries act as a compass, guiding you toward choices that resonate with your authentic self.

**Embody Gratitude:**

Gratitude is a guiding force in mindful decision-making. Regularly express appreciation for the opportunities, experiences, and relationships in your life. A grateful heart fosters a positive mindset, influencing decisions that emanate from a place of abundance rather than scarcity.

Cultivate a daily gratitude practice, acknowledging the blessings in your life. As you navigate decisions, this attitude of gratitude becomes a lens through which you view challenges. By recognizing the positive aspects, even in difficult situations, you empower yourself to make decisions rooted in optimism and a sense of abundance.

**Adaptability in Decision-Making:**

Life is dynamic, requiring flexibility in decision-making. Cultivate adaptability, allowing your choices to evolve as circumstances change. The ability to pivot with grace and resilience ensures that mindful decision-making remains relevant in the ever-shifting landscape of life.

Embracing adaptability involves cultivating a mindset of acceptance and openness to change.

Reflect on past decisions and their outcomes, extracting lessons that contribute to your adaptability toolkit. In doing so, you equip yourself with the skills to navigate unforeseen challenges and pivot toward decisions aligned with your evolving goals.

**Share Your Wisdom:**

As you embark on this journey of intentional living, share your wisdom with others. Mentorship and guidance create a ripple effect, inspiring those around you to embrace mindful decision-making. Your experiences become a beacon for others seeking clarity and purpose in their own lives.

Consider establishing mentorship connections or participating in knowledge-sharing forums. By imparting your insights, you not only contribute to the growth of others but also deepen your own understanding of the principles guiding mindful decision-making. The act of sharing wisdom fosters a sense of interconnectedness and community.

**Embrace the Journey:**

Finally, embrace the journey itself. Mindful decision-making is not a destination, but rather a continuous process of self-discovery and growth. Celebrate the small victories, learn from the challenges, and relish in the beauty of crafting a life that reflects your authentic self.

In weaving these additional threads into the fabric of mindful decision-making, we amplify the richness of our personal narratives. The dance of life becomes more intricate, more intentional—a symphony of choices that resonate with purpose and clarity. As we embrace this transformative journey, let us continue to explore the depths of our mindful intentions, crafting a life that is not just lived but profoundly experienced.

Before I end this chapter, I want to reflect on the journey of my generation as I am reminded of the remarkable women who were pioneers of mindful decision-making, paving the way for a new understanding. One such influential figure is Oprah Winfrey, whose insights continue to resonate, serving as timeless reminders for us all.

Two pillars stand out prominently in Oprah's teachings: power and choice. She emphasizes the sacred privilege of choosing one's own path, recognizing that everyone's journey is unique and filled with challenges. As Oprah wisely puts it, "Understand that the right to choose your own path is a sacred privilege. Use it. Dwell in possibility."

Life and courage come together to form the second cornerstone of Oprah's wisdom. Acknowledging the nuances of life requires time, devotion, and discipline. Embracing vulnerability and confronting fears are essential steps toward transformative change. Oprah beautifully encapsulates this truth: "Mindfulness tells us when we go beyond the superficial and conventional understandings of our habitual patterns, when we look deeper and enlarge the scope of our vision, we develop a wiser relationship with all aspects of our experience."

Incorporating these principles into our lives is not a one-time endeavor, but rather a daily practice. Much like meal prepping and exercising for physical well-being, nurturing our minds and thoughts demands constant attention. Our upbringing and societal conditioning have shaped us, instilling certain patterns of thought. It is crucial to recognize that adopting mindfulness practices, such as daily meditation and a shift in thinking, can bring about profound joy and inspiration.

I encourage you to consider the most powerful practice of empowering a better version of yourself. Take the time to integrate these mindful decision-making principles into your daily life. The journey of self-discovery and empowerment is an ongoing process, one that requires dedication and a genuine commitment to cultivating a wiser, more intentional relationship with life's unfolding experiences. Expanding your conscious awareness and intentionality will lead to a more profound connection with your choices, shaping a life that aligns with your truest self.

In certain cultures, storytelling is considered medicine—an art of being present and speaking intimately with an audience of one from the heart. It stands as one of the oldest and deepest forms of human communication. Combine mindfulness practices with your own traditions or spirituality, working to understand how to connect and make decisions with impact. My hope for you is to find solace and lead your life purposefully. May your journey be one of continual growth, wisdom, and the joyous fulfillment of your intentional pursuits.

# Chapter Thirteen
## Embracing Authenticity in Social Media
## By Michelle Perkins

Michelle Perkins is a seasoned social-media manager with a passion for amplifying brands' online presence. With a focus on crafting engaging content and visuals tailored to target audiences, Michelle is dedicated to optimizing social-media strategies.

Her mission revolves around the creation and execution of tailor-made social-media strategies that align with your unique business objectives and effectively connect with your audience. Through careful management and optimization of your social-media channels, she ensures your online presence consistently reflects your brand's essence, and her data-driven approach enables her to continuously fine-tune strategies for sustained success.

Her track record speaks volumes about ability to deliver results. She has significantly expanded organic reach and boosted engagement for the brands she's worked with, making a positive impact in the digital realm. She is always in tune with the latest trends and innovations.

    www.instagram.com/michellerperkins
    www.tiktok.com/@michellerperkins

# Embracing Authenticity in Social Media

*By Michelle Perkins*

In the bustling world of social media, where every entrepreneur vies for attention, the golden key to standing out is simpler than one might think: authenticity. As a social-media coach, I've navigated the choppy waters of what works and what doesn't, and time and again, the truth rings clear: being the real you is not just beneficial, it's essential for business success—especially on platforms like Instagram, Twitter, LinkedIn, or any space where you choose to engage online.

Authenticity is about more than just the occasional behind-the-scenes snapshot or sharing personal stories now and then. It's about weaving your true self into every fabric of your online presence. This isn't just about posting; it's about creating a narrative that resonates on a deeply personal level with your audience. It's a continuous commitment to transparency, honesty, and genuine interaction that defines a successful online persona.

## The Crux of Authenticity

Think about who you like to follow online. Is it the people who constantly showcase a perfect, unattainable lifestyle, or those who aren't afraid to share the real, unpolished aspects of their lives? The answer typically leans towards the latter. That's because, at our core, we crave real connections. Authenticity allows you to become more than just another face in the crowd; it transforms you into someone relatable, trustworthy—a figure that people can believe in. In the realm of business, where trust is the currency, being genuine is invaluable.

### The Magic of Being Yourself

The magic of authenticity is that it empowers you to stand out in the crowded digital landscape. No one else has your unique story, your voice, or your style. Leveraging this uniqueness helps you cut through the noise effortlessly. Being yourself attracts the right kind of people—your people—to your brand.

And the truth of the matter is that you do not want the wrong people attracted to your brand.

For example, when I first started my social-media-management business I really wanted to get as many clients as I could. So, I started out undercharging for my services.

What I didn't realize was that it would attract a type of clientele that was not my ideal client. And then they would refer more clients to me because I was so inexpensive. The challenge was that I wasn't being true to myself.

I found that I would put aside my own time to live my life and handle even the smallest things for them that were beyond the scope of our contract.

I would coach them on what to put on their website, even their own business practices like operations. Then, when I figured out all the time I was spending with them, I started to realize I wasn't generating a profit in my business.

I wasn't being authentic to myself or my clients. In fact, it got really hard for me because my clients then **expected** me to do so many things out of the scope of the contract, it started affecting my health.

What I learned was I had to not only embrace being true to myself and living authentically, I also had to set boundaries and expectations with my clients.

For example, I had one client in particular who would text me at all hours of the day and night, and on the weekends. She expected me to answer her right away and would act upset when I didn't answer on the weekends.

One Sunday when I was at church, she texted me. I decided not to respond until Monday. She was livid with me and very condescending. It was then that I realized I wasn't being true to myself—or her, for that matter.

I was doing her a disservice by modeling inauthentic behavior and not having boundaries in place. I decided to have a conversation with her the following Tuesday to give her time to calm down.

She listened and was still upset. She continued to expect me to not only show up on her schedule but to post items on her social media that were not congruent with her real behavior.

I couldn't do this anymore. So, I gave her a 30-day notice to discontinue our service. The day I did was the day I realized that I had to value my authenticity and be more mindful about how I conducted my business.

Another lesson I took away from this experience was that I wanted clients who were mindful of how they treated themselves and other people. I also wanted clients who showed up the same way on social media they did in their lives.

From that day forward, I began identifying the characteristics of exactly who my ideal clients were. It felt so good! Then, I began calling them in.

The interesting part about all of this is that when I set my intentions and then surrendered them to the divine, my ideal clients began showing up.

All because I began embracing who exactly I wanted as clients: authentic entrepreneurs.

**Embracing Authenticity**

So, how does one embrace authenticity? Begin with your story. Share the genuine journey of your business—the highs and the lows. It humanizes your brand, making you more approachable. Interaction is key; don't just speak at your audience, speak with them. Create a community around your brand by engaging in meaningful conversations.

Moreover, don't shy away from being seen as you are. The need for constant perfection is a myth. Sharing real moments from your daily life or work, including the bloopers, adds layers to who you are. It reveals your genuine self.

**The Challenges of Authenticity**

However, being open and real opens you up to potential criticism. Not everyone will understand or appreciate your authenticity and that's perfectly okay. Your goal isn't to appeal to everyone but to find your people—those who resonate with what you do and stand by you.

**Deepening the Connection**

Talking like a human, not a robot, is crucial. Use language that you would use in real conversations. This approach makes your content more relatable, fostering a sense of friendship and trust. Embrace the messy parts of life and business openly. Sharing your struggles and the lessons learned not only showcases honesty but also resilience—a trait every entrepreneur needs.

Your social media should celebrate your community. Your followers are more than just numbers; they're part of your journey. Make them feel included by sharing their stories, highlighting their posts, and creating a sense of belonging. This cultivates a platform where real connections thrive.

Staying true to your values is non-negotiable. If you're passionate about something, let it shine through your social-media presence. This authenticity attracts people who share your values, building a community based on shared beliefs.

Continuous learning and evolution are part of being authentic. Share your growth, the new things you're trying and how you're adapting. It demonstrates a commitment to improvement and can inspire others on their journey.

Let your unique personality shine through. Whether you're humorous, serious, or anywhere in between, your personality is what sets you apart. Embrace it fully.


**Beyond the Basics**

Authenticity extends to the visuals you share. Opting for real, unfiltered images over heavily edited ones invites your audience into your world, making your brand's story and values more tangible.

Being prepared to respond to criticism with grace is an essential part of authenticity. How you handle negative feedback can turn potential setbacks into opportunities for growth and connection.

Leveraging authentic influencers can amplify your message in a way that feels organic and genuine, introducing your brand to new audiences naturally.

Consistency across platforms reinforces your brand identity, making it easier for your audience to connect with you, regardless of where they find you.

Encouraging user-generated content fosters a sense of community and serves as authentic endorsements of your brand, showcasing real-world validation of your brand's value.


**The Authenticity Feedback Loop**

Authenticity is a feedback loop that involves listening to your audience, adapting based on their feedback, and continuously evolving. This engagement strengthens the trust and relationship between your brand and its community.


**Conclusion**

In essence, authenticity on social media is about being human. It's about showing up as you are, embracing imperfections, and celebrating the journey. This approach not only attracts more clients but also builds a loyal community around your brand.

Remember, people connect with people, not faceless brands. By infusing authenticity into every aspect of your social-media strategy, you create a brand that's not only successful but also deeply resonant and meaningful. In a digital world clamoring for attention, the most remarkable thing you can be is yourself, ensuring not just growth but a lasting impact.

Living life on purpose means being authentic and mindful in everything you do, including what you share on social media.

# Chapter Fourteen
## The Road to Wealth in a Weekend
## By Amanda Moxley

A manda Moxley is an international business coach, author and speaker with nineteen years of experience. Amanda is best known for helping her clients create "wealth in a weekend." While most business coaches help their clients have six-figure years, Amanda coaches her clients to have six-figure paydays. Amanda is the creator of the "Wealth in a Weekend" challenge, which walks you through how to assemble your audience, turn your words to wealth and generate a year's worth of income in a weekend through the power of profitable live and virtual events, retreats and workshops.

www.instagram.com/amandajmoxley/

www.facebook.com/healthandwealthcoach
www.amandamoxley.com
www.tiktok.com/@amandajmoxley1234
https://www.twitter.com/AmandaMoxley
www.wealthinaweekendworkshop.com

# The Road to Wealth in a Weekend

*By Amanda Moxley*

**Let's take a trip in my time machine back to 1977…**
It was the year my parents **got divorced**.
**I was just two years old**…
The separation ended up **creating a deep well of feeling unloved, unworthy, and unwanted.**
(*That wasn't their intention, of course…and I have done the work to forgive and have massive compassion for them.*)
A few years ago, I started doing a little bit of research on my family's past. (One key thing in being an entrepreneur is knowing that your WC1 (wounded child) can get in the way of your WC2 (wealth consciousness) and if you don't consciously decide to rise up, you can keep repeating patterns that keep you stuck vs. leaning into your power and making money!)
I found out that, when my dad was twelve years old, his baby sister was born.
But the sad part was, she came into this world with a complication that kept her at just five pounds.
After five years of silent battles, the precious baby passed away, *and my family did what they knew best:*
**They buried their pain, moved away, and cloaked their memories in silence.**
Fast-forward to 1975, when I was born.
And guess who didn't come to my birth?
Yep.
My dad didn't show up (which I now have compassion for based on his childhood). He chose a day of skiing.
Perhaps the ghosts of the past held him more tightly than the promise of the future…
Well, that didn't work out for my parents.

So, when I was just **six weeks old, they put me into a daycare with a loving family.**

Since my childhood was a little rough, you might imagine my road was rocky.

And you'd be correct.

I ended up going to a super-strict school where I was one of two kids in my class from a broken home.

My response to my family's fractured fairy tale?

Behavioral problems.

But the answer I received wasn't one of comfort or understanding.

You see, this was in the early 80s...

And the way my teachers dealt with my troublemaking?

They cast me out of the classroom, and they put me in a dark, dank, scary closet.

I vividly remember being inside the closet in the first grade—feeling so afraid, ashamed, and abandoned.

I felt so unworthy.

Fast-forward to high school.

I was drinking and partying a lot and getting into fights here and there.

Then there was this really cute guy named Jason.

One day, as we were sitting on the grass waiting for the bus home, he asked me, *"Amanda, what do you want to do with your life?"*

I just started talking:

"I want to live a life of freedom...have a soulmate...be married...be a mom...and be able to be home with my kids!" I exclaimed.

"I want to make enough money that I don't have to go to work!"

Jason seemed a little taken aback by my clear vision.

And that's what I like to help my clients with.

Having a clear vision helped me achieve my goals.

I broke free from the closet, got crystal clear on my goals, and ***out of my pain and shame came my fame***.

So, what about you?

What is it you truly desire in your heart of hearts?

What pain have you personally been through that you want to re-package to help other people—and profit from?

You can turn your words to wealth, assemble your audience, and sell.

As a speaker, author, and coach...

As someone who's sharing and leading other people through your experiences...

You need to become present with those pockets of pain and share them in a way that will allow others to be set free from their own similar situations.

I call this your "seminar story."

## A Single Event Changed My Life

Ever had an event that you just had to go to no matter how badly your bank account was drained?

This happened to me.

I said to myself, "I don't care what it takes, I need to figure out how to be a million-dollar coach and entrepreneur. I'm never going back to my job as a therapist."

So, I flew from Utah to California and stayed in this nasty hotel in Venice Beach.

I distinctly remember sitting in the hot seat telling the coach my sob story...

"I'm down to my last $200. My mom had to help us pay our mortgage."

What she said to me next put me on my path.

She said, *"Amanda! You're in your messy middle. You're going to share this someday. This isn't your end."*

In that moment, a wave of relief washed over me. I saw myself on **stages** getting **paid** to share my story to help others.

It was the most freeing thing ever.

I had felt so ashamed for so long.

(Remember the dark, dank, scary closet?)

I chose to take my power back.

She invited me into her $10,000 program where I would take the actions to become the person who could **hold** my vision.

All I had to do was make a very powerful decision that day: was I ready to get off the sidelines of my life and fully step into my power and **claim** my dreams?

Even though I didn't have the money, I instinctively said, "Yes."

I thought, "I'm already this low down to $200. What's another $10,000? When my real goal is 2 million?"

Luckily, I had my plastic sponsor in my purse: my American Express credit card.

It was one of the biggest gambles I'd made—I had decided to back myself and do what needed to be done.

I remember my mentor saying, "**God's got your people**."

I decided to put my **faith** into action. I put together my signature talk, raised my rates, and stretched myself by following up with prospects and asking for the sale.

And guess what?

In six short weeks, I had made $54,000!

I wasn't even selling a business offer.

At the time, I was a health coach, transforming people's lives helping them move beyond their body barriers.

In those six weeks, I enrolled eleven clients at $5,000 each.

That was huge for me as, prior to my coaching, I'd only charged a maximum of $1,800.


Here's what I learned:

- It's harder to make a lot of money in a long amount of time.

- It's easier to make a lot of money in a short amount of time.

This sounds counter-intuitive, but I'm living proof this works.

The bottom line?

Collapse the time frame by drawing your line in the sand and decide to **go for it!** Raise your rates, tell your story, and sell your programs for the lifetime value of the transformation you provide. Think bigger.

**The Man Who Ruined My Mascara**

After I started to gain traction, my mentor asked, "Amanda, do you want to join my $100,000 program?"

Now, the obvious answer was.

"Duh, of course."

But let's get real.

I was barely pulling myself out of debt as it was.

I had just made back my investment, and I was afraid of pulling the trigger at $100,000.

So, when facing a big situation, I did what I thought many people would do…I went to church.

The worship leader with a **deep** voice was singing, *"Your desire… is the key…that opens the door…"*

*"Your desire… is the key… that opens the door…,"* he continued.

Without a moment's notice, tears were streaming down my face.

**"My desire is the key that opens that door."** I kept repeating to myself.

I was crying and crying. Mascara was dripping down my face.

I knew in my heart of hearts what my desire was.

"I really do want to do that $100,000 program and meet the version of me who claims her desires."

Since I'd only made $50,000 a year before, this was two years' worth of income; it was a stretch.

But I got resourceful, figured out how to make it happen, bet on myself again, and wrote that check.

You see, the first step to wealth in a weekend is **desire**.

Once you allow yourself to own your desire, you'll be able to unlock the money, audience, opportunities, influence, and more.

So, what is it you truly desire?

Deep inside of you.

Think about it and write it down.

The second step to wealth in a weekend is **decision**.

Decision is where the rubber meets the road.

This is where you draw the line in the sand.

Decision literally means "to cut off at the root."

So, what do you need to let go of?

What boundary do you need to put up?

What do you need to say **no** to?

Raise your standards. Stop tolerating.

Answer these and start making decisions fast with confidence.

Trusting your gut instead of overthinking things is usually what money loves.

So, decide with all your heart.

Once you do, what ends up happening is the whole world moves with you!

The third step to wealth in a weekend is **drive**.

This is all about you taking action.

Once you know what you desire, and then you've made your decision, now it's time for you to drive toward your goal.

My story ends well: I bet on myself despite the challenges of my childhood and I multiplied that $100,000 seed (with God's grace) to over two million dollars!

I learned how to host my own profitable events that generated a year's worth of income in a weekend.

We got to move into our dream home and spend three summers living on the beach in Hanalei, Kauai while raising two gorgeous kids, and being in love with my soul-man, Johnn. We all are very close to my amazing parents and get to ski together as a family.

Give it everything you've got—work with a mentor and you'll see how much further (and faster) you could really go!


Love,
   Amanda Moxley

# Chapter Fifteen
## Look Inside Yourself, The Answer Is There
## By Nicole Toney

Nicole Toney is a dedicated professional with a passion for personal development and education. She holds a master's degree in Psychology and a bachelor's degree in Human Resource Management, showcasing her commitment to both the human psyche and effective organizational management.

With a diverse background, Nicole has worn many hats in her

career journey. Her experience spans from her early days as a public-school teacher, where she helped shape young minds, to her roles as a corporate trainer, guiding individuals and organizations towards success. Nicole's expertise in human resources has equipped her with the skills to navigate the complexities of workforce management, ensuring that people are at the heart of every organization's success. Her work as a mental-health case manager further reflects her dedication to the well-being of others.

Beyond her professional life, Nicole is a multifaceted individual. She finds joy in the simple pleasures of life, such as reading, cooking, and traveling, which not only enrich her experiences but also allow her to connect with different cultures and perspectives. Most importantly, she cherishes spending quality time with her family, where she finds love and inspiration.

As an entrepreneur, business consultant, life coach, and mentor, Nicole Toney continues to make a positive impact in both the corporate world and the lives of those she guides. Her unwavering commitment to personal growth and her genuine passion for helping others achieve their full potential define her as a truly inspirational figure.

www.linkedin.com/in/nicoledtoney/

https://www.facebook.com/profile.php?id=100084066543648

# Look Inside Yourself, The Answer Is There

By Nicole Toney

Living mindfully and authentically is a path to greater self-awareness, inner peace, and genuine connection with the world around us.

Mindfulness is the practice of being fully present in the moment, paying attention to our thoughts, feelings, and sensations without judgment. It requires deliberate effort and can be cultivated through techniques such as meditation, deep breathing, and simply slowing down to appreciate the present.

Authenticity is the alignment of our actions, words, and values with our true selves. It's about living in a way that reflects our inner beliefs and desires rather than conforming to external expectations or societal norms.

To live mindfully and authentically, we must first embark on a journey of self-discovery. This involves introspection and self-reflection to gain a deeper understanding of our values, passions, and what truly matters to us. Journaling, therapy, and meditation are valuable tools in this process.

Once we have a clearer sense of self, mindfulness practices can help us stay attuned to our inner world. Daily meditation, even if it's just a few minutes, can train our minds to observe thoughts and emotions without attachment. This awareness can prevent us from reacting impulsively and instead respond thoughtfully to life's challenges.

Mindfulness extends beyond solitary practices. We can apply it to our daily activities, such as eating, walking, or working. By giving our full attention to these activities, we savor the richness of life's experiences and enhance our connection with the present moment.

Living authentically means making choices that align with our values and passions, even if they defy societal expectations. It requires courage and vulnerability to be true to ourselves, but the rewards are immense. Authenticity fosters deeper connections with others, as people are drawn to those who are genuine and transparent.

Another crucial aspect of living authentically is embracing imperfection. We must recognize that we are not infallible and that mistakes are an integral part of growth. This self-compassion allows us to be more forgiving of ourselves and others. Sometimes we can be our own worst critics, so be honest with yourself but don't be cruel and unforgiving.

Authenticity encourages us to set boundaries and say "no" when necessary. By doing so, we honor our own needs and protect our well-being, which ultimately benefits our relationships and overall happiness.

Living mindfully and authentically is a fulfilling way to navigate life. Here's a guide to help you on this journey:

**1. Self-Reflection:**

- Take time to reflect on your values, beliefs, and goals.
- Understand your strengths, weaknesses, and areas for growth.

**2. Mindfulness Practice:**

- Develop a daily mindfulness practice, such as meditation or deep-breathing exercises.
- Stay present in the moment, appreciating each experience without judgment.

**3. Authenticity:**

- Embrace your true self, acknowledging your uniqueness.

- Be honest with yourself and others about your feelings and intentions.

## 4. Gratitude:

- Cultivate gratitude by regularly acknowledging the positive aspects of your life.
- Keep a gratitude journal to record moments of appreciation.

## 5. Minimalism:

- Simplify your life by decluttering physical and mental spaces.
- Focus on what truly matters and eliminate distractions.

## 6. Connection:

- Nurture authentic relationships with people who support your values.
- Practice active listening and empathy in your interactions.

## 7. Self-Care:

- Prioritize self-care activities that rejuvenate your mind, body, and spirit.
- Set boundaries to protect your well-being.

## 8. Intentionality:

- Live with purpose by setting clear intentions for your actions.

- Align your daily choices with your long-term goals and values.

## 9. Acceptance:

- Embrace imperfections in yourself and others.
- Understand that growth often comes from challenges and setbacks.

## 10. Continuous Learning:

- Be open to new experiences and ideas.
- Seek personal growth through reading, courses, or pursuing new hobbies.

## 11. Compassion:

- Practice self-compassion and extend it to others.
- Understand that everyone is on their unique journey.

## 12. Nature and Mindful Movement:

- Spend time in nature to connect with the world around you.
- Engage in mindful movement like yoga or tai chi to enhance body awareness.

## 13. Patience:

- Recognize that change takes time.
- Avoid rushing through life; savor each moment.

## 14. Disconnect:

- Take breaks from technology to reduce distractions and reconnect with the real world.

**15. Mindful Eating:**

- Savor your meals by eating slowly and appreciating the flavors.
- Listen to your body's hunger and fullness cues.

Remember that living mindfully and authentically is a continuous journey. It's about finding harmony between your inner self and the external world while staying true to your values and principles. Be patient with yourself and enjoy the process of self-discovery and growth.

Self-discovery and fulfillment are deeply personal journeys that vary from person to person. Ask yourself this question: "How well do I know myself?" It can be scary getting to know yourself because you may find out things about yourself that you're not pleased with, but the good thing is that you can change. Don't feel like you're stuck and have to continue being what you have been if you're not happy with that person. Many times, we find ourselves repeating the same cycles that we are trying to heal from, but we don't know how to change. Here are some steps that may help you in your quest:

1. Self-Reflection: Start by spending time on self-reflection. Ask yourself meaningful questions about your values, interests, passions, and what truly makes you happy.

2. Explore Your Passions: Try new things, explore hobbies, and engage in activities that genuinely interest you. This can help you discover your passions and what brings you joy.

3. Set Goals: Establish clear and achievable goals for yourself. These goals can be related to your personal growth, career, relationships, or any area of your life that you want to improve.

4. Mindfulness and Meditation: Practicing mindfulness and meditation can help you become more aware of your thoughts,

emotions, and inner self. It can also provide a sense of peace and clarity.

5. Learn from Challenges: Embrace challenges and setbacks as opportunities for growth. They can teach you valuable lessons and resilience.

6. Seek Support: Talk to friends, family, or a therapist about your journey. Sometimes, an outside perspective can provide valuable insights.

7. Help Others: Often, helping others and being of service can bring a sense of fulfillment. Volunteer work or acts of kindness can be deeply rewarding.

8. Continuous Learning: Never stop learning. Whether it's through books, courses, or experiences, continued learning can lead to personal growth and self-discovery.

9. Embrace Change: Be open to change and adaptability. Sometimes, your path to self-discovery may lead you in unexpected directions.

10. Set Intentions: Clearly define what kind of people you want in your life and what you want to achieve through these changes.

11. Identify Toxic Relationships: Recognize any toxic or negative relationships that may be holding you back. This can be friends, family, or acquaintances that bring you down.

12. Create Boundaries: Establish healthy boundaries with those who may be causing your stress. This may involve limiting contact or ending certain relationships.

13. Find Like-Minded People: Seek out new friendships and social groups that align with your goals and interests. Join clubs or organizations related to your hobbies.

14. Stay Positive: Cultivate a positive mindset and focus on your future rather than your past.

15. Practice Self-Compassion: Be kind and forgiving to yourself. Self-discovery can be a challenging process, and it's important to treat yourself with compassion along the way.

16. Patience: Understand that change takes time. Be patient with yourself as you navigate through these shifts in your life.

Remember that living mindfully and authentically is a lifelong journey of self-discovery and self-expression, it's perfectly normal for it to evolve over time. It requires commitment, self-compassion, and the willingness to step outside our comfort zones. Yet, the rewards are profound—a deeper connection to ourselves, more meaningful relationships, and a richer experience of life. By practicing mindfulness and embracing authenticity, we can cultivate a life that is truly our own, filled with purpose and fulfillment.

I found that practicing mindfulness helps me to stay present in my daily life. By being authentic about my feelings and priorities, I've built stronger connections personally and professionally. This shift positively impacted my well-being and relationships, highlighting the transformative power of living mindfully and authentically. What brings you fulfillment may change as you grow and learn more about yourself. Be patient and open to the possibilities that lie ahead. Starting today, choose you and keep choosing to be the best version of yourself—not only for yourself, but also for your family, your friends, your career, and whatever else you are a part of. Choosing you doesn't mean "**only me**", it means "**me too**." You are your own kind of awesome and nobody else can be you, so when you show up make sure you show out!

# Chapter Sixteen
## Yin and Yang, All at Once
## By Dr. Katy Chang

Dr. Katy Chang is a board-certified nurse practitioner, certified yoga instructor, certified mindset and manifestation coach, and certified energy healer.

Her life's work has been to help others, initially as a nurse practitioner and now empowering others as a mindset and manifestation coach. Dr. Katy has helped thousands around the world step into their greatness by identifying root issues, healing from past traumas, and creating a new reality centered around positive thinking. She believes that to master your life, you must master your mind. Her methodologies focus on channeling disempowering thoughts into empowering thoughts and actions. Her clients learn how to transfer that energy in their favor to move the needle forward in their life or business. As the sole creator of your reality, are you ready to start manifesting what you want in life? Let Dr. Katy show you how!

www.linkedin.com/in/dr-katy-c-7652799a/
www.instagram.com/drkatychang/
www.facebook.com/doctorkatychang
www.drkatychang.com/
www.tiktok.com/@drkatychang

# Yin and Yang, All at Once

*By Dr. Katy Chang*

Dedicated to Mandy Morris and Oliver Niño, you have expanded my world, my life and my purpose. I am living out my authentic purpose because of you. And for my Tiktokers, I am humbled and honored; you have given me a reason to live!

Every single one of us has dealt with a moment in our lives where we felt stuck—hopeless that there were no other options for change, that was it, that was all life is ever going to be. Just because you feel stuck doesn't mean you are. Just because your client feels stuck doesn't mean they are. Stuck is a feeling, and the feeling of being stuck stems from focusing on the wrong problem; the reason you're not seeing the results you want is not due to a lack of solutions or knowledge, but rather due to mindset. There is a wealth of knowledge at our fingertips through the power of the internet. There are endless coaches, programs, and books for us to consume. The "stuckness" and stagnancy that we see in our lives, especially in our businesses, comes down to our *mindset*. I am here to tell you that everything you desire in life can be yours, that there is a solution. You are simply a mindset shift away from manifesting anything you want in life; whether that's health, wealth, or a relationship.

After overcoming multiple challenges in my life, and having taught thousands around the world, I noticed a common theme: the pendulum, when released, always has to swing to the opposite direction. That's the constant. Everything in life has a yin and a yang, a black and a white. This reliable polarity is a constant.

When you feel hopeless or "stuck," rest assured the pendulum must swing in the opposite direction (that is the only option for a pendulum). When you give it energy, your pendulum will swing from your human story of limitation to your divine story of possibility. My goal for you in this chapter is to give you the mindset tools to challenge your perceptions so that you can live out your life in the divine, soulful story where you can be, do, and have anything you want in life.

**Love Vs. Fear**

Love versus fear, or light versus heavy, is a concept I use to shed awareness on whether I am making a decision from my human story, a.k.a. fear, or from my divine story, a.k.a. love. Our intuition is always guiding us to choose the authentic and divine path, the one that is centered on love; it's our north star. However, we often choose just the opposite: to stay in our human story. Out of fear, we choose the *heavier* path because it's safe and comfortable even when our internal compass is screaming for us not to. We ignore our intuition; we make decisions out of fear and we wonder why our life does not look the way we want it to look or be. Why do we continue to ignore our intuition and choose a place of inauthenticity even when there are clear signs directing us towards the light?

The answer is past programming.

**Past Programming**

We choose to live in a state of inauthenticity due to fear from past programming. Our lives are shaped by subconscious beliefs that were programmed into us during the first seven years of our lives: programs of limitation, disempowerment, and self-sabotage. These programs were acquired from other people, such as our parents or societal constructs, and not from ourselves. And these beliefs that we have been programmed to believe continue to influence us 95% of the time. In other words, 95% of the decisions you make in life aren't stemming from thoughts that are authentically yours; they are from someone else, a learned behavior or pattern that influenced you from a young age. These programs are occurring without conscious recognition and awareness; they're deeply rooted in our subconscious.

That is why it's often difficult to follow our north star, to choose a path outside of fear—because the human story is what we have grown up with and are accustomed to. It's familiar. We struggle to manifest our conscious mind's wishes and desires due to our subconscious programming sabotaging us into our fear-driven patterns and beliefs.

Is there an area in your life that isn't going as desired right now? Can it be due to past programming and operating from a place of fear rather than from a place of love? From this point moving forward, it's time to get curious when a thought feels vibrationally heavy. Ask yourself, "Is this fear really mine? Who is speaking? Who else in my life do I know that speaks or thinks like that? Is that thought really mine, or does it sound like someone I know?" The goal here is to deconstruct the past programming so you can peel back the layers of your inauthentic self to reveal the authentic self of who you really are. Get curious without judging yourself.

**Triggers: The Good, the Bad and the Ugly**

We've all had them, events occur that trigger responses in us. Just like there is a yin and a yang, there are good and bad triggers; however, we are more familiar with the bad triggers as they elicit responses from us that cause a splitting of multiple personalities. These multiple personalities can be defined as different personas that happen at the time of an event; they are a whole other person that is birthed out of the triggering event. A large number of our triggers stem from past programming, the inauthentic parts of us that have not been seen or heard before but that get to be heard once triggered. Triggers occur as opportunities for expansion—to expand and grow as a human being. When we are triggered, it's an opportunity to look within at the part of us that still needs to be healed as we wouldn't be triggered if we didn't feel some sort of threat to our safety, to ourselves and to our spirit by the other person.

## T.T.E.A.R. and C.S.I.:

Trigger → Thoughts/Beliefs → Emotions/Feelings → Actions → Reality

T.T.E.A.R.

A triggering event sets off a chain reaction that shapes our reality. Thoughts and emotions branch off from the triggering event, e.g., we often feel anger from a trigger. From our emotional state we react and take action that will produce an outcome that affects our present and future reality. I call this the T.T.E.A.R. Effect.

If you want things to change in your life, you must think and feel different thoughts. If you continue to be triggered as you have always been, think as you have always been, believe as you have always been, then nothing in your reality will change. Life is always in motion, so you cannot be "stuck." The "stuckness" is rinsing and repeating the same energies and patterns from your beliefs and expecting a different outcome; that's the definition of insanity.

As you can see from the T.T.E.A.R. Effect, you are the creator of your own reality. Your thoughts and emotions point toward your future reality; you are never stuck with your current reality. Just because you have picked up thoughts, beliefs, and patterns from past programming does not mean that you have to continue attracting a response to them. You have the power to control your own human experience by catching, stopping, and interrupting (C.S.I.) the thoughts that aren't authentically yours and choosing a different chain reaction by being mindful of your thoughts. Continue to get curious and be mindful of your triggers and the personas that are birthed from those triggers. Ask yourself, "Is the persona or personas I'm currently in helping me manifest my dream life? Do they belong in my future? Does this serve me to where I want to be? Are the personas and their patterns constructive or destructive to my future reality?"

## Where There's the Yin, There's the Yang: Mastering the Divine Story

If we are the creators of our own reality, and we created our present reality from past programming, then how do we create a different reality from a place of authenticity rather than inauthenticity, from love rather than fear, so we can truly be, do, and have anything we want in this life?

Where there's yin, there's yang. Where there's black, there's white. If there are "bad" triggers, can there be "good" triggers? What if I told you we can get ahead of the curve by actually eliciting positive triggers? Most of our stress and problems stem from us operating in the wrong persona for the issue at hand. So, we must *consciously* choose to operate in the positive and correct persona for the problem we are looking to solve.

Instead of allowing the "destructive" persona to appear after a trigger, why not release the "constructive" persona to get the job done? Is there a project you've been putting off? Why not call upon your do-er persona to get started on the project? Is there a relationship you want to patch or draw closer? Why not call upon your heart-open and heart-centered persona to be vulnerable and connected to people?

There is a more divine, elevated persona for us to tap into, to work to our advantage. Start calling upon those beautiful parts of you to create not just the life you want but the life that you truly deserve.

# Chapter Seventeen

## Social Comparison ~ WE Will Not Conform to the "Norm"

### By Jennifer Kiser

I have a passion for movement, nutrition, fitness, wellness, and have been led to guide family, friends, and community since adolescence. I possess a master's in health science from Logan Chiropractic University, and I am an alternative medicine clinician, physiologist, kinesiologist, nutrition coach, performance coach, mindset coach, program coordinator/writer, master life coach, author, and educational-motivational speaker with focus on identity, trauma, self-esteem, body image, and confidence (specifically to empower women). I am a bodybuilder, bikini-division competitor, model, and coach. I have created and designed a beauty brand that will be on the market in 2024; the brand name is Chroma, and the brand slogan is "confidence is beautiful" because I believe it is!.

I love to be involved with women-empowering groups. All women who are empowering are also empowered! I feel so fulfilled and blessed to be living a life of purpose, on purpose.

www.linkedin.com/in/jennifer-kiser-816992230
www.instagram.com/jkmastercoaching
www.facebook.com/JenniferKiser

# Social Comparison ~ WE Will Not Conform to the "Norm"

*By Jennifer Kiser*

Living up to social and professional standards of today requires demands and pressures that create anxiety and stress overload. An *everyday woman's* approach to managing conflicts and environmental stressors greatly impacts the ability to fulfill tasks and may have short-term and long-term physiological, cognitive, social, emotional, and performance effects. In a professional setting, one is often expected to manage emotions and exhibit appropriate demeanor, even during confrontational scenarios. The management of displayed emotions often requires self-regulation and can create emotional strain. Emotional dissonance, or lack of emotional harmony, occurs when suppressing emotion. Suppressing emotions results in an internal threat to one's own identity. Professionals who experience stress from emotional dissonance utilize more energy and likely develop emotional exhaustion. Once reaching emotional exhaustion, regulating emotions becomes difficult and, if left unaddressed, stressful encounters could result in a break in character, depersonalization, and cynicism.

*Social comparison theory* was initially proposed by a social psychologist, Len Festinger in 1954. This theory expresses the evaluation of an individual who compares oneself socially to measure and self-evaluate, identifying personal standards vs. the beliefs and standards of others. Media, social status, influence, and other comparisons may affect our physiological and psychological being. According to the *social comparison theory*, focusing on social comparison for self-enhancement may expand or suppress emotional beings.

*Everyday women* of today's culture are not only required to manage the home and family, but also social and professional roles. What ignites motivation yet provides guidance to live a life of authenticity and mindfulness? Is it practical to live a life of authenticity and practice mindfulness in tandem?

In this chapter, I will share a practical outline for how to live a life of both *authenticity and mindfulness.*

*Authenticity*

*Everyday women* may live a life of authenticity by discovering connections among self-esteem, goal-achievement, and coping skills. Authenticity involves the ability to practice, introspect, and understand what motivates oneself. This is an ongoing process developed based on one's own personality, spirit, values, and beliefs, regardless of environmental pressures. Evaluating and discovering self-knowledge may reveal uncomfortable truths or weaknesses that one may prefer avoiding; however, it is more favorable to be accurate and honest rather than biased. An authentic person's validation is derived from adhering to an internal compass which is sufficient for their mental well-being. Philosophically speaking, authenticity is considered the genuine, true, original state of human existence, which is often described as a life of freedom, joy, meaning, value, and happiness. Developing authenticity is an ongoing lifelong journey of moving from transformation to transformation. The process of self-discovery requires time and patience. Due to every individual's unique personality, identity issues, health issues, traumas, self-worth, and physiological design, there is no specific time stamp for developing and evolving.

*Key Factors to Creating an Authentic You*

- Identify Your Values
- Identify the Discontinuity
- Communicate Honestly
- Live with Integrity

- Develop Self-Confidence
- Don't Make Assumptions
- Manage Your Emotions

**Identify Your Values.** Living *authentically* means that you live according to your core beliefs and values, followed by framing personal goals which emerge from them. Once core values and beliefs are identified, one may begin committing to living and working in accordance. Ensure that your personal and career goals align with your core beliefs and values.

**Identify the Discontinuity.** Bridging the gap from your current *self* to the future you will require identifying current behaviors followed by linking goals to the vision of your future. You may identify your gaps by writing a list of words that describe the person you intend to be, in reflection of the person you are today. Begin to practice one word at a time by using personal *goal-setting* tools, and evolve by practicing intentionally daily. Remain focused on one task at a time, setting small goals, one by one. Managing progress toward a goal in small, consistent measures leads to more successful outcomes.

**Communicate Honestly.** Honesty requires quality communication skills and emotional intelligence. Honesty involves communicating with clear, direct, concise direction while respecting the feelings and conditions of the other person. Honesty is adhering to the fairness, facts, or uprightness of character or action.

**Live with Integrity.** Integrity is the firm adherence to a code of artistic values or morals. The ability to develop and preserve integrity requires courage. Living a life of integrity requires taking responsibility for your actions, including mistakes. Admit your mistakes and work continuously to change your shortcomings.

**Develop Self-Confidence.** Being assertive and developing a strong sense of *self* is a key component to building *authenticity*. Living *authentically* requires strength of character, especially when pressured by others to act in a particular fashion that may be out of your character. Confidence is a feeling of self-assurance arising from the appreciation of your own abilities or qualities. Practice daily affirmations of self-love, dress confidently, and be confident!

**Don't Make Assumptions**. Allow others to speak and share their beliefs without judging. Genuinely listen to other people, respecting their personal thoughts and feelings. Extending an open-minded approach to others may allow reciprocated, equal respect and courtesy to you.

**Manage Your Emotions.** Living *authentically* requires managing emotions during difficult situations and conversations. Developing skill to control emotions is an important component of living a life of *authenticity*. Demonstrating the ability to control emotions during difficult conversations reveals that you have inner strength and respect for others. Emotional maturity will serve you well in all facets of your life and career.

Living a life of *authenticity* provides a number of benefits, including the ability to realize your own potential, respect from others, and genuine happiness/well-being. Authenticity is living your life in accordance with your personal desires, values, and beliefs regardless of what friends, family, and society may expect from you.

*Mindfulness*

Everyday women may live a more fulfilled life by developing an understanding of, and then practicing, *mindfulness*. To live mindfully requires living in the moment and reawakening yourself to the present, as opposed to dwelling on the past or anticipating the future. *Mindfulness* is the process of objectively observing and labeling thoughts, feelings, sensations in the body. Therefore, *mindfulness* can be a tool to avoid self-criticism and judgment while identifying and managing challenging emotions. *Mindfulness* is used frequently during meditation and therapeutic settings. Practicing *mindfulness* offers benefits including protecting against depression and anxiety, lowering stress levels, and reducing harmful ruminating. *Mindfulness* may also offer the benefits of increased ability to cope with rejection and social isolation, and improving quality of life.

*Mindfulness Encompasses Two Key Components*

- **Awareness: Awareness is the** ability to focus attention on one's inner processes and experiences, such as the experience of the present moment (e.g., my feet feel the soft, fluffy, warm blanket).
- **Acceptance:** Acceptance is the ability to observe, receive, and accept streams of thoughts rather than judge or avoid them.

The purpose of meditation practice is to simply meditate, remaining in the moment without distractions. The goal while practicing meditation is to allow all thoughts that are generated to pass through your mind without judgment. Focusing on being centered with yourself and remaining aware of your breathing rhythms will help with "grounding." Meditation begins and ends in the body, and it involves taking the time to become aware of your orientation, and what you are feeling, smelling, hearing, and/or seeing. Practicing the act of awareness and acceptance can be calming as our body has internal rhythms that commune with these practices.

The Mindfulness-Based Stress Reduction (MBSR) program was designed in 1979 by an American professor of medicine, John Kabat-Zinn, who developed the program at the University of Massachusetts Medical School. This practice was derived from a combination of Buddhist principles, Hatha yoga, and mindfulness.

*Benefits of MBSR*

- Pain management
- Increased sense of well-being
- Improving brain health
- Slowing brain aging
- Improving quality of life for those with chronic conditions
- Reducing stress, anxiety, and depression symptoms
- Improving cognitive ability
- Improving immune response
- Improving symptoms from sleep disorders
- Relief from digestive disorders
- Balances hormones levels

Practicing mindfulness is not limited to utilizing the MBSR technique. In addition to MBSR, there are numerous meditation practices to focus on your specific demands. Therapeutic modalities incorporate mindfulness as well. Holistic therapy offers an umbrella of modalities that offer specific benefits. Holistic therapies include cognitive behavioral, dialectical behavioral, somatic, ecotherapy, reiki, hypnosis, and breathing techniques.

*How to Practice Mindfulness*

- Write in your journal.
- Enjoy a cup of tea.
- Watch the sunrise or sunset.
- Take a walk.
- Listen to classical music.
- Go stargazing.
- Do a hands-on craft.
- Cook with a new recipe.
- Get a manicure or pedicure.
- Take a pottery class.
- Get a massage.
- Plant flowers.
- Practice Yoga.
- Sit by a fire.

Mindfulness cultivates and recognizes the best of who we are as human beings, as *everyday women*.

Everyday women feel personal, social, and career pressures of today's culture, yet we have the power to control thoughts and actions by practicing *authenticity* and *mindfulness*. Everyday women will gain independent power back through these practices. Be sure to be true and honest with yourself, protect your identity, and live *confidently* and *authentically*. Stay grounded, be happy!

# Chapter Eighteen
## Success Redefined: Thriving Beyond Limits
## By Stephanie Freiboth

Stephanie Freiboth is a trailblazer in the pursuit of helping you ditch traditional views of what career success "should look like", trading up for a ridiculously rewarding career that is aligned to your priorities. She has worked with Fortune 50 and private companies advising, coaching and motivating executives and their teams to up-level their professional potential by leveraging their networks, building relationships and improving mindset. Her secret sauce? A high-energy, no-nonsense style that challenges conventional thinking and focuses on what truly matters in both work and life.

www.linkedin.com/in/stephanie-freiboth-032a2b4/
www.instagram.com/stephanie.freiboth/
www.facebook.com/stephanie.freiboth
www.myempoweredcareer.com

# Success Redefined: Thriving Beyond Limits

*By Stephanie Freiboth*

SUCCESS...charming, enticing, sexy, nefarious, elusive, evolving.

As women, it's a concept we proudly pursue, while simultaneously finding it challenging to navigate conflicting priorities and circumstances of our career and personal lives.

Success isn't just about corner offices, six-figure paychecks, or fancy job titles. It's about finding your sweet spot. You know it. It's that place where your heart does a happy dance and your soul feels nourished. It's different for everyone, which is precisely what makes it so fascinating.

In the relentless pursuit of ambition, do you find yourself entangled in the complex dance of your own expectations and the echoes of others' perceptions? Does success for you become an unyielding force, demanding more and more of you with every decision? In this very personal and intricate give and take, it is inevitable that aspirations will collide with life circumstances, causing an internal struggle that will leave you exhausted if you don't tend to it.

The beauty of success is that it's yours to define. It's about what makes your heart sing, your eyes sparkle, and your spirit soar. It's not about comparisons with others whom you perceive to have more than you. From a co-worker who got the job you wanted to social media validation, it can feel like a constant borage of messages to work harder, get more, and do more without any consideration to what is going on in your personal life.

Take a walk with me. Our concept of success is intimately linked to the seasons of our lives and the experiences that consume our energy, time, and emotional capital.

In *youth*, it's filled with the innocence of endless possibilities. Success often revolves around making our parents proud, excelling at school, fitting in, and gaining independence.

As we venture into *adulthood*, success may shift to career, financial security, and the pursuit of personal goals. It's a time of building, a season of ambition and achieving milestones.

The *midlife* season often prompts us to reflect on the success we've achieved and reassess our priorities. Success may mean finding fulfillment and purpose beyond material accomplishments. Then, in the *later years*, success may evolve into a more contented state. It might involve sharing wisdom, cherishing relationships, and leaving a legacy.

Through all of this we are experiencing joy and tragedy. There is a high probability you have experienced one or some of the following: marriage, divorce, childbirth, infertility, raising children, addressing your own serious illness, helping a loved one through their serious health condition, or caring for aging parents. These are just a few examples of life circumstances that affect how you feel about your career and what you expect out of your employer and your loved ones.

Here's the million-dollar question: when one of those life-changing experiences happened, did you pause to evaluate what will change in your life as a result and what that will require of you?

Success for you in one season of life might be working extra hours and saying "yes" to special projects outside of your core work to gain experience and build your professional brand. Then you may transition into crafting a work-life balance that lets you savor family dinners without late-night shifts. You may decide to launch that passion project that has been in your heart because now you have the financial means you didn't have earlier in your career. Or perhaps it's a career transition to a different industry because your children are now more independent.

Let's break down four factors influencing your definition of success:
### 1. Managing Expectations and Chasing Dreams
Expectations, both internal and external, play a significant role in

shaping our concept of success. In our youth, the expectations are often set by others—parents, teachers, or society. We strive to meet those expectations, sometimes losing sight of our own desires. Success is tied to fulfilling these predefined roles. As we grow and gain independence, we start to chase our own dreams, breaking free from the expectations of others. Success becomes a pursuit of personal aspirations. Yet, it's also a time when external pressures, like societal standards or the opinions of others, can weigh heavily on our decisions.

## 2. The Perceived Value of Others' Opinions

The opinions of others can be a double-edged sword in defining success. On one hand, external validation can boost our confidence and affirm our choices. On the other, it can lead us to question our own path if it doesn't align with the expectations of society or loved ones.

Early on, peer approval may shape our sense of self-worth, impacting what we believe constitutes success. As we mature, we learn to weigh external opinions against our own values and desires. Ultimately, we realize that success is a deeply personal journey, and external validation, while nice, should not be our sole measure of it.

## 3. Life Events and the Ebb and Flow of Success

Life is unpredictable, marked by a series of events that can redefine our understanding of success. A promotion, a family crisis, or a personal epiphany can lead to shifts in our perspective and priorities. These events act as chapters in our success stories, each shaping our definition in unique ways. A promotion may seem like the pinnacle of success at one point, while a family crisis can shift our priorities, emphasizing the significance of balance and well-being. Personal epiphanies, like realizing we're on the wrong career path, prompt us to redefine success by following our passions and purpose.

### 4. Factors Influencing Self-Perception

Our self-perception, a cornerstone of our definition of success, is influenced by various factors, including our self-esteem, self-efficacy, and personal growth. The more we learn, grow, and experience, the more our self-perception evolves.

In our youth, we may struggle with self-esteem and be highly influenced by societal standards. As we age, we often become more confident, knowing ourselves better, and having a more accurate assessment of our capabilities and worth. This evolution influences how we define and pursue success.

Success is not an absolute measure but rather a personal barometer. Imagine it as a weathervane that shifts with the winds of life. This analogy reminds us that success is dynamic, like the weather—ever-changing and influenced by various factors. The seasons of our lives, the events we encounter, and our self-perception all contribute to the direction to which our success weathervane points. It's a constant adaptation to shifting priorities, just as our definition of success adapts to the seasons of our lives.

## Tips for Navigating the Ever-Changing Path to Success

- **Be Proactive:** Assess your goals and aspirations early and often. Think ahead, anticipate changes, and adapt your definition of success accordingly. Flexibility is key.
- **Balance Expectations:** Strive for a balance between internal and external expectations. Define success based on your values and desires while considering external feedback as valuable input, not a mandate.
- **Pivot Sooner:** Don't be afraid to pivot when the situation calls for it. Sometimes, recognizing that your current path doesn't align with your evolving definition of success is the first step toward achieving it.

- **Knowledge Exchange:** Embrace the wisdom and experiences of others. Seek out mentors and engage in continuous learning. It helps you anticipate changes and make informed choices.

You will experience changes in your life that require you to modernize your definition of success. Go from surviving to thriving when you prioritize this proactive approach to reflection and action.

Use this simple template to give you a visual representation of your current goals, values, priorities, and life circumstances, allowing for a clearer understanding of the adjustments that need to be made. Regularly revisit and update this to track changes and ensure your life aligns with your evolving definition of success.

**Priorities:**

- Identify and write down the key priorities in your life during the current stage. These could include aspects like family, career, personal development, health, etc.

**Goals:**

- Jot down specific goals related to the identified priorities. These could be short-term or long-term objectives that align with your current life stage.

**Values:**

- Articulate the core values that guide your decisions and actions. These could include principles such as integrity, growth, compassion, etc.

**Rate Satisfaction (1 to 5):**

• Rate your satisfaction with how well your current life aligns with the corresponding priority, goal, or value. Use a scale of 1 to 5 (1 indicating low satisfaction and 5 indicating high satisfaction).

| List Priorities | Rate (1 to 5) | List Goals | Rate (1 to 5) | List Values | Rate (1 to 5) |
|---|---|---|---|---|---|
| | | | | | |
| | | | | | |
| | | | | | |
| | | | | | |
| | | | | | |

What themes do you see and what is out of alignment?

What is your definition of success in this season?

What do you need to ask help with and who will you ask?

# Chapter Nineteen
## Turning Soft Confidence Into Hard Evidence
## By Sami Lei

Sami dreams of a world where anyone can achieve success, regardless of what cards they're dealt in life. To contribute to this dream, she runs a management-consulting firm helping small business owners and startup founders with analytics, strategy, and operations to grow their revenue so they can invest money instead of time into their business. She also offers personal development, business, and executive coaching.

Sami loves helping people find their path in life, make decisions that make sense logically and emotionally, and say "yes" even when it's scary. She makes time for meaningful relationships, life adventures, and her cats. She has learned how much she receives by giving, and she hopes to spend the rest of her life making authentic connections from which everyone involved gets meaningful value and happiness. And above all, she wishes you a beautiful and blessed life.

www.linkedin.com/in/sami-lei/

# Turning Soft Confidence Into Hard Evidence

*By Sami Lei*

Some people are just born with confidence. Some people learn it. And some people need hard evidence to believe in themselves—I'm one of those people.

I was raised in a home with parents who wanted the world for me. Like many parents at the time, they expressed this by highlighting the achievements of others. I tried to point out that the reason such feats were even discussed was because they were so spectacular and out of the ordinary that most people would be unable to achieve them. This logic fell on deaf ears.

I didn't realize they just wanted the best for their daughter.

They didn't realize they were crushing my self-confidence.

I lied to myself, pretending I didn't want to achieve those things anyways. But in reality, I was afraid that if I tried, and didn't yield the results my parents wanted and would be eager to brag about... that failure would be more painful than never trying at all.

Lack of confidence bred fear—a wall of fear I didn't think was possible to overcome. Thankfully, three things occurred that transformed my mindset and helped change the way I looked at myself.

-----

### 1. I found a dream, passion, something I genuinely cared about.

When I was fourteen, my father was working in a different state. Given how often he was gone from home, choosing next to start a business on a different continent didn't seem like that big of a difference. So, he did.

We didn't have money or connections, so starting a business was hard. My dad had high hopes of creating a successful business for us children to inherit one day, but he succumbed to a scarcity mindset. Ten years passed without much business growth, and my mom wanted him to come home.

Seeing his journey unfold, I became fascinated by business. I wanted to learn how to build big businesses and grow them quickly and efficiently, so that even people who weren't born into wealth could succeed.

I applied for startups I didn't meet the requirements for, because what if they let me in? I accepted roles I wasn't confident I would succeed in...because what if I did?

I overcame fear because I was more frightened that I would fail to get future opportunities than I was of failing the first time.

I overcame fear because I found something I cared about.

-----

## 2. *I learned that I was worth it, and my dreams and happiness were worth it.*

After college graduation, it became a yearly ritual for me to ask myself "Why don't you start your own business?" And for years, I had an answer.

- I was still young.
- I was learning so much from being at a top management-consulting firm.
- I would never be allowed to run a business while holding my current job and I don't want to get fired.
- No one would trust a girl who looks like she's fourteen with their business strategy.

At some point, I really thought my corporate success would lead to some sort of confidence, some belief that I was good at business. I kept waiting for the day I would wake up and be confident in my capabilities.

It took ten years for me to realize that wouldn't happen if I didn't ask the right question: "If not me, who?"

I had ten years of experience in strategy and operations. In management consulting. At Fortune 500 Companies. Early-stage to late-stage startups. Running and closing my own business. My question morphed: "If not now, when?"

And then came the breaking point. I wondered, "If these accomplishments are possible because of my capabilities, should I stay in corporate or start my own business helping people like my dad grow their businesses quickly instead of spending decades away from their daughters?"

I cried.

I lamented the years I waited on the sidelines, not choosing to start my own business. I justified that I was actually exactly where I needed to be and I needed all that time to learn and have experiences that would make my company what it is, and make me who I was.

And then I said "yes." I started my management-consulting business, my first full-time business—with no salary to keep me safe.

Because if I failed, giving myself this chance was still worth it. And if I succeeded, I absolutely deserved it.

-----

Since then, I've built a framework to analyze that situation, and every other decision my heart and my head disagree on. I've included this framework below so it can help you, too.

You see, I believe that people make decisions through logic and emotion. Some lean on one more than the other, but if both agree, the decision feels irrefutably correct. I use this analysis now for anything that makes me feel lost, whether it's determining what business ideas are worth pursuing or figuring out if I'm doing the right things with my life.

For this example, I'll use the question "Was I right to start this business?"

|  | Quantitative | Qualitative |
|---|---|---|
| Logical | <ul><li>220 businesses helped in Y1</li><li>$1000 donated to benefit the startup community</li><li>Built network of 500+ business owners in Y1</li></ul> | <ul><li>Revenue > expenses, with extra to reinvest</li><li>Unique opportunities to meet people, travel to conferences and grow personally</li><li>Ownership of my time and energy, unlocking flexible and effective freedom of work</li></ul> |
| Emotional | <ul><li>Built more financial models in the last 12 months than I have in past 10 years</li><li>220 business owners got access to talent, expertise, and insight at price points that have never existed to small business owners or startup founders</li><li>Enabled 50+ families to stop viewing personal sacrifice as the only way to grow their business</li></ul> | <ul><li>Built a business where I wake up feeling energetically aligned and blessed to bring businesses revenue using the tactics I traded ten years for in corporate</li><li>Pushed myself personally to become a stronger version of myself to be able to support all the people I wanted to help</li><li>Designed option to decrease the sacrifice early founders, like my dad fifteen years ago, have to put in to achieve success</li></ul> |

I started this business because I was passionate about helping early-stage entrepreneurs bet on themselves and start their own business.

I started this business because I believed I deserved a chance to be the change I wanted to see in the world.

### 3. If I can find a moment where my belief in myself outweighs my fear, I can gather the evidence I need to shake off that fear in the future.

In my youth, I didn't realize:

- I was already successful and phenomenal.
- It's possible to have so much to learn **and** to already be amazing.

- When faced with an opportunity I wasn't confident I would succeed in, I had chosen so many times to try anyway.

With each success, each failure I learned from, each "what doesn't kill you makes you stronger," I was adding wins to my victory chart.

I was finding evidence that I could be successful, evidence I should be a little more confident in myself.

And now, with the personal growth running my own business brought me, I recognize that I had the power to look each opportunity in the eye and say "If I bet on my success today, and I'm right, what else does that unlock?"

Wayne Gretzky once said, "You miss 100% of the shots you don't take." What he didn't mention is how taking one shot can open the door to so many more.

The real cost of not taking the shot isn't that you miss one chance to make one shot. It's never learning how many shots you could make, not seeing how far you could go, not getting the wins on the board to one day form the foundation of evidence-based confidence.

-----

Today, I still don't view myself as a confident person. And I'm still scared of many things, especially failure.

But I now have a mountain of evidence that I can run a business, and I have the mindset, skillset, and frameworks that allow me to logically and emotionally think through decisions for my life, my business, and my clients.

On the other side of fear are the dreams we all have for ourselves. The dreams we all know we deserve. There may be a moment of soft confidence, a moment of belief that we might be capable enough, belief that we might deserve success, belief that our love for something is worth it.

In those moments I choose to trade my soft confidence for evidence, to take that moment—that opportunity that comes from feeling fear—and choose to do something anyway. I choose to come out on the other side with irrefutable proof that I can achieve the dreams I set out to achieve.

# Chapter Twenty
## How To Outsmart the Distractions
## By Amy Elizabeth

Amy Elizabeth is a wife, mom, "grammy," retired nurse, travel agency owner, and accredited success coach who loves seeing the world, spending time with family, and advocating for animals.

When she's not working or volunteering, you can also find her reading, gardening, meditating, and snorkeling. She has also lent her voice to multiple projects as a voice-over actress.

She and her family reside in Texas.
www.instagram.com/thetravelbossmom
www.Facebook.com/successcoachamy

# How To Outsmart the Distractions

*By Amy Elizabeth*

It seems like we live in a world full of distractions.

From television to world events and hectic daily schedules, it all seems to be an endless cycle of looking here instead of there and not doing what we need to do to be centered in our lives.

Even in homes, you will find families gathered around each other with their faces glued to a phone instead of looking at the people who mean the most to them.

So, how can we change the dynamic?

How can we get past social media, the electronics, and everything else, and get back to being mindful of what we *should* be paying attention to?

It is truly my hope that in these next few pages, you find a new way to organize and simplify your life and once again allow the world to flow around you versus you trying to fly around like a blind bird.

Before we go further, let's look at what being mindful entails.

Being mindful is an elevated state where we are observers. We pay attention to things with no distraction from everyday hustle and bustle.

Let's say you have a goal and a set of tasks needed to complete that goal.

When you absolutely have to complete the goal, there is nothing that can deter you from completing those tasks. So, you are being mindful of your goal. Simple, right?

Maybe in black and white. However, we live in a world of color. **A lot of color**.

And we are part of that beautiful prism with our own authentic selves, so we want to put our own twist on things. This is where things get a bit convoluted. Most times, this is also where we become easily distracted and overwhelmed. Now we must figure out how to not only be more mindful of situations and circumstances, but also how to authentically add ourselves to the mix. Well, this can be a chore to most, but I am here to tell you that **you can** make this happen!

You need to stop. And breathe. This can be done at any point and at any time.

Stopping means putting away your phone. Turn off all electronics. Walk away from it all and literally just breathe.

(This won't be forever because there is work to do.)

Take ten minutes.

Focus on **you** in the moment.

Close your eyes. Listen to your breath sounds as you inhale and exhale. Feel your heartbeat.

The first step in being more mindful of **everything** is learning to be mindful of yourself and where you are in this chaotic world.

When we step away from distractions, we allow ourselves to exist and become enveloped by the energy of peace we create. In a sense, we stop time for just a moment and give our minds and spirit a break so we can process what we need to truly focus on.

Once you have come back to a place of centering and focus, you may notice that you can see things more clearly.

Your mind has moved through the fog of emotion and distraction, and you can find exactly what you had been looking for that alluded you (like finding your glasses on top of your head when you've hunted all morning for them!)

Once you have successfully become more mindful of yourself, which you need to do **daily**, how can you begin to implement this into your daily life and subsequently build your own success stories?

I want you to read and reread this:

**When we align our energy with the universe first, then create a balance in our relationships, our work and success stories will ultimately follow naturally.**

So, the next step is to create a *mindful balance* in our relationships.

This means scheduling time for our loved ones.

We all have twenty-four hours a day.

Trust me when I say you can turn off social media for a few hours and spend quality time with those you care about, whether they be family, friends, your dog. Whomever it may be, schedule time **for** them.

You will notice I say "for" versus "with" because "with" entails just being present. They need more than a warm body. They need **you** and your attention. You are giving the gift of yourself to them. So, spend that time being there **for** them.

And make this a group project; everyone turns off their phones and is just living in the moment.

You will be amazed at the memories you can create when you all participate!


Once you have **consistently** begun creating a happy bubble of mindful energy in your personal life, you may also begin noticing that your professional life is changing for the better.

Why would this be?

Some of the biggest distractions in the workplace include problems at home or with your health. By building on the foundation of becoming self-aware, you are more conscious of your health, and more satisfied with those around you in your personal circle. Doing this actually erases the *distractions* of unhappiness and chaos outside of the workplace to allow you to focus on the tasks you need to complete each day! (What a concept that is!)

Remember when I said to reread that saying above?

Go back and read it again.

Seriously.

I'll wait...

It makes more sense now doesn't it?

Sometimes the biggest distractions come from within and *allow* our minds to be distracted by the world around us.

When we start and continue to bring balance to ourselves, we begin to bring balance to our lives.

We shift our mindset.

And shifting these gears doesn't just bring our daily lives into balance, but it also gives us a new perspective on ourselves.

We begin to realize who we are as individuals.

**Whoa now**—plot twist!

Let's dive deeper, shall we?


I mentioned above that we live in a world filled with colors. Blinding and beautiful, like a prism in the sunlight, we are all part of a harmonious balance of color and life.

However, when we get distracted, our light can get distorted and even dimmed.

This wasn't how we were meant to live.

Our light is meant to be blinding and beautiful.

So, how can we once again be as we were meant to be?

You have already read the first step.

That is to become more mindful of yourself.

When you do this, you shift our view back to the person who we were created to be.

You will begin to realize more deeply your quirks, habits, strengths, and areas for growth.

Then you can begin to work on them.

This starts a chain reaction in your daily life.

You'll see errors and achievements that you used to dismiss because you were too "busy" to notice them before.

You'll begin to fix yourself and celebrate yourself.

You will also start to become mindful of how you treat others.

This will allow your light to shine a little brighter each day.

Finally, you'll empower others to do the same for themselves.

Remember, that like a moth to a flame, when your light begins to shine brighter, others will be attracted and want to know how you have gotten to where you are.


Now, realize that this is not an overnight story. Or even a one-week exercise.

This is an every-single-day practice that eventually becomes a habit.

So, this is what I want you to do after you've read this.

Turn off all your electronics.

Find a quiet space.

And breathe.

Be grateful for the air as it enters your lungs and expel all negativity as it leaves you.

Hear your heartbeat.

Be grateful for the blood that passes through your body.

Then *focus* on three things that matter the most to you in your personal life.

Those are the things you need to bring balance and attention back to so you can move forward and past the distractions of each day.

The things you need to bring balance and attention back to can include your spouse, your kids, your home, your parents—whatever they may be, they *need* you.

Continue to breathe and focus on the **positive** memories you have of these three things.

Allow yourself to feel the emotions associated with them because, in the end, we are all emotionally driven.

Then when you have given it about ten to fifteen minutes, get into your calendar and clear time **for** those three things.

Begin making time for them.

And when you are with them, be there **for** them.

Allow yourself to be present in the moment.

Do this for a few weeks not just in your personal life, but in your professional life as well!

I look forward to celebrating your beautiful light with you!

# Chapter Twenty-One
## My 9 Step Comprehensive Plan
## By Dr. Vicki D. Coleman

D r. Vicki D. Coleman is a former tenured professor at Purdue University in West Lafayette, IN, and a bestselling author. She has held positions at the State University of New York, Educational Testing Service, and American Airlines. Dr. Coleman is an internationally recognized behavioral health clinician, and functional and integrative medicine expert. She speaks globally on a variety of topics, such as depression, PTSD, career development, and sports psychology.

A certified federal mediator, she engages with individuals, families, and organizations to facilitate the resolution of anger and conflict. Her research includes self-concept/self-esteem, anger management, gerontology, sports psychology, and multicultural and diverse populations.

Dr. Coleman earned a bachelor's in political science from The University of Iowa, a master's in U.S. & Latin American history from The University of Iowa, a master's in counselor education from Northern Illinois University, and a doctorate in counseling psychology from Rutgers University in New Brunswick, NJ.

www.LinkedIn.com/in/doccole
www.Instagram.com/AngerDoctor
www.Facebook.com/DrVickiDColeman
www.AngerDr.com
www.TikTok.com/@DoccoleAnger
www.Twitter.com/DrVicki

# My 9 Step Comprehensive Plan
*By Dr. Vicki D. Coleman*

## **INTRODUCTION**

To live mindfully and authentically, I believe, is the fundamental principle for total health and wellness, including being satisfied and happy in the global economy.

Living mindfully and authentically indicates that we must be initially and fully aware of our self-concept and self-esteem, which are the perceptions that we have of ourselves, and how we feel about ourselves, respectively. And living mindfully and authentically by focusing on self-care, self-concept, self-esteem, and career development can facilitate a life of being able to make positive, satisfying, and appropriate decisions, among other things.

Living mindfully and authentically in the global economy requires us to be aware of the implications and repercussions of the myriad values, core beliefs, cultures, economies, and social and political systems, including the similarities and differences in how we live.

Consider utilizing the following 9-step comprehensive plan to achieve a lifestyle of mindfulness and authenticity.

## **THEORETICAL FRAMEWORK AND ORIENTATION**

My theoretical framework and orientation is related to self-concept and self-esteem and has its philosophical underpinnings in the work of Dr. Donald E. Super, et al. (1963) and Dr. William H. Fitts (1964, 1996). Both were psychologists who made a significant contribution to the field by establishing theories, frameworks, orientations, definitions, and assessment instruments.

Super, et al. (1963) examines self-concept and the feeling tone, self-esteem.

Fitts (1964) & Fitts & Warren (1996) divide the self into six categories, which became the theoretical foundation for the Tennessee Self-concept Scale (1964); and the Tennessee Self-concept Scale-2 (Fitts & Warren, 1996).

I have modified the Fitts' six areas of self-concept and self-esteem to develop the Coleman model of self-concept and self-esteem (2008; 1992), which also includes the work of Super, et al. (1963).

The aforementioned research has become the foundation of my research and clinical application of self-concept and self-esteem, among others.

## **SELF-CONCEPT AND SELF-ESTEEM**

Self-concept is the perception that we have of ourselves or what we *think* about ourselves; and self-esteem is the "feeling tone" of self-concept, or how we *feel* about ourselves (Super, et al., 1963).

Self-concept is the perception that we have of ourselves as individuals, including values, core beliefs, world view, personality traits and characteristics, strengths, abilities, skills, interests, talents, and areas for improvement, to name a few.

As self-concept and self-esteem are not one construct, I subscribe to—and modified—the six areas of self-concept developed by Fitts & Warren (1964, 1996), illustrated in their classic, global self-exploration inventory, the Tennessee Self-concept Scale (TSCS):

- Personal self-concept and self-esteem
- Physical self-concept and self-esteem
- Family self-concept and self-esteem
- Social/community self-concept
- Academic/work/professional/financial self-concept and self-esteem
- Moral/ethical/spiritual self-concept and self-esteem

Below is a more detailed description of the six areas of self-concept and self-esteem.

I consider these six areas of self-concept and self-esteem when focusing on a Mindfulness and Authenticity Plan, including establishing goals (Fitts & Warren, 1964, 1996; Weihman, 2023).

1. *Personal self-concept and self-esteem*
   - Values, core beliefs, world view

2. *Physical self-concept and self-esteem*
   - Physical, physiological, body image

3. *Family self-concept and self-esteem*
   - Biological family of origin, others identified as family

4. *Social/Community self-concept and self-esteem*
   - Friends, neighbors, city, county, state, and country, global relationships

5. *Academic/Work/Professional/Financial self-concept and self-esteem*
   - Education, colleagues, professional, financial

6. *Moral/Ethical/Spiritual self-concept and self-esteem*
   - Ethical, legal, spiritual considerations, why are we here, reason for being

Understanding self, in each of the above areas of self-concept and self-esteem, is the initial step in identifying, developing, and implementing a plan related to mindfulness and authenticity in the global economy.

## CAREER DEVELOPMENT

The Coleman model of career development (Coleman, 2008; Coleman & Barker, 1992; in Giles & Ventura-Rozen, 2021) is the paradigm and framework that I utilize and recommend when addressing the issues, concerns, and challenges related to living mindfully and authentically in the global economy.

However, it is important to consider that career development is a *process,* and not to be completed in one engagement or session.

Career development may often require intervention from a qualified, competent professional.

## COLEMAN MODEL OF CAREER DEVELOPMENT

1. Introduction and orientation
2. Self-assessment
3. Decision making
4. Educational, occupational, and community information
5. Preparation for the world of work, leisure, and retirement
6. Research and evaluation

*1. Introduction and Orientation*

An introduction to the concept and process of career development and vocational psychology is the initial step. Career development is an ongoing, lifelong process that focuses on the acquisition of information and skills focus on self and the environment.

*2. Self-Assessment*

This step requires an in-depth assessment and evaluation of one's self-concept, self-esteem, values, core beliefs, interests, abilities, strengths, personality, goals, and world view, among others.

*3. Decision Making*

There are several models that highlight the decision-making process, including various steps, strategies, and styles. What is critical is that individuals can discern themes, trends, and patterns related to how they make decisions and ask the question, "Are my decision-making strategies and styles affording me the opportunity to make positive, satisfying, and appropriate decisions?"

4. *Educational, Occupational, and Community Information*

With technology, there is a wealth of information related to any topic, and we can use information to determine the requirements for our educational and occupational backgrounds, including the community resources that can facilitate our success.

5. *Preparation for the World of Work, Leisure, and Retirement*

In the 21$^{st}$-century global economy, individuals can plan and prepare for the workplace, leisure, and retirement at the same time. Often, retirement means leaving one career and entering another, including entrepreneurship.

6. *Research and Evaluation*

Upon moving through the aforementioned career-development process, it is important to *review* the process, determining whether previous steps should be reconsidered. Also, as an academician and clinician, it is critical that I can provide evidenced-based information and resources for my clients and patients.

## 9 STEPS TO MINDFULNESS & AUTHENTICITY

### 1. Self-care

*Practicing self-care is paramount. And we **must** take care of ourselves first, prior to being able to help or assist others!*

*What are the implications of self-care with respect to living mindfully and authentically?*


### 2. Self-concept and Self-esteem

*Self-concept and Self-esteem provide the foundation for surviving in the global economy. Ask yourself, "Who Am I?" with respect to the perception and feelings related to the six areas of self-concept and self-*

esteem: personal, physical, family, social/community, academic/work/professional/financial, and moral/ethical/spiritual?

What are the implications of self-concept and self-esteem with respect to living mindfully and authentically?

## 3. Values, Core Beliefs, and World View

What is important to you? What are your core beliefs? How do you engage with others? And what are your beliefs related to surviving in the global economy?

What are the implications of values, core beliefs, and world view with respect to living mindfully and authentically?

## 4. Decision Making

Do you understand the steps in the decision-making process? What are your decision-making strategies and styles?

What are the implications of decision-making with respect to living mindfully and authentically?

## 5. Information

How do you gather information, and from what sources? How do you utilize technology to gather information? How do you discern the efficacy of the information obtained?

What are the implications of information with respect to living mindfully and authentically?

## 6. Relationships

*What are the myriad relationships that you experience, such as personal, family, work, community, etc.?*

*What are the implications of these relationships with respect to living mindfully and authentically?*

## 7. Anger and Conflict Resolution

*How do you handle the emotion of anger? What are your fundamental communication skills? How do you resolve conflict?*

*What are the implications of anger and conflict with respect to living mindfully and authentically?*

## 8. Career Development

*The ongoing, lifelong process of examining self, decision-making, information, and preparation for work, leisure, and retirement, among others.*

*What are the implications of career development with respect to living mindfully and authentically?*

## 9. Global Competency

*Being culturally aware of the myriad people, groups, and communities who comprise the global economy is critical, including how we are all connected and related.*

*What are the implications of the global economy with respect to living mindfully and authentically?*

## BARRIERS

Barriers are obstacles that prevent us from getting what we want, doing what we want, and achieving our goals.

**Barriers Can Be Internal or External:**

**Internal Barriers** are those within us and are easier to identify and control; examples include low self-concept, low self-esteem, or fear.

**External Barriers** are those outside of us, are not easy to identify and control (if possible at all), and are related to the environment, including the global economy.

## Internal Barriers:

- *Lack of confidence*
- *Frustration, fear, anxiety, or mental disorder*
- *Low self-concept and/or low self-esteem*
- *Lack of specific skills and abilities*
- *Lack of understanding of relationship with the healthcare system*
- *Cultural expectations*

What are the implications of internal barriers with respect to living mindfully and authentically?

## External Barriers:

- *Global economy*
- *Lack of opportunity*
- *Healthcare crisis and limitations*
- *Stereotypes and discrimination*
- *Local economy and environment*
- *Cultural implications*

What are the implications of external barriers with respect to living mindfully and authentically?

## **SUMMARY AND CONCLUSION: LIVING MINDFULLY AND AUTHENTICALLY IN THE GLOBAL VILLAGE**

In the $21^{st}$-century global economy, there are myriad issues, concerns, problems, and challenges that we encounter on a daily basis.

Living mindfully and authentically can create a framework for how we address the daily stressors of life.

I have proposed a 9-step plan for living mindfully and authentically.

# References

Coleman, V.D. (2008). *A model of career development: 21$^{st}$ century applications.* Australian Career Practitioner, Spring, 19, 19-20.

Coleman, V.D. & Barker, S.A. (1992). *A model of career development for a multicultural workforce.* International Journal for the Advancement of Counseling, 15, 187-195.

Coleman, V.D. & Barker, S.A. (1991). *Barriers to the career development of multicultural populations.* Educational and Vocational Guidance, 52, 25-29.

Coleman, VD. (2023). *Dare to Care: Focus on Self-Care, 1$^{st}$. In Weihman, M.R.* Dare to Care: Healthcare Superheroes Share Stories of Resilience, Hope & Inspiration. ISBN-13979-8988427803.

Fitts, W. (1964). Tennessee Self-concept Scale (TSCS). *Los Angeles, CA: Western Psychological Services.*

Fitts, W. & Warren, W.L. (1996). Tennessee Self-concept Scale 2$^{nd}$ Edition (TSCS-2). *Los CA: Western Psychological Services.*

Giles, A. & Ventura-Rozen, Galit. (2021). Be Your Own Superhero. *In the Everyday Woman's Guide to Doing What You Love. Heart Centered*

*Women Publishing (HeartCenteredWomenPublishing.com)*

Porter, H. (2018). 40/40 Rules: Wisdom from 40 Women over 40, Volume II. *Washington, Utah: Prosperity Publishing.*

Super, D.E., Starishevsky, R., Matlin, N., & Jordaan, J.P. (1963). Career development: Self-Concept theory. Essays in vocational development. *New York, New York: College Entrance Examination Board.*

# Chapter Twenty-Two
## Coaches Empower Individuals to Maximize Their Potential
## By Nalo Thomas Mitchell

Nalo Thomas Mitchell received a bachelor of arts in broadcasting from the Walter Cronkite School of Journalism at Arizona State University, a masters from Colorado Technical University, and is pursuing a doctorate in Theology. This anointed woman of God believes that when you're steadfast before The Lord, you'll learn that you are an amazing masterpiece, born in the right place at the right time. She is the proud wife of Pastor Darrell Mitchell; together they founded #NWPNM in 2020, and on January 21, 2024 launched New Victories International Ministries. Together they have four children and five beautiful grandchildren. As an ordained pastor, prophetess and a three-time national and international best-selling anthology author, Prophetess Nalo has made a name for herself in different fields. With a twenty-year career in education, she has excelled by making others feel inclusive and loved through a lens of equity. Her passion for helping others see the best in themselves and reach their goals is truly inspiring. If you're looking for someone who can help guide you on your journey, Prophetess Nalo is willing to help!

www.linkedin.com/in/nalo-thomas-mitchell-msm-67969a62/
www.instagram.com/nalo_thomas_mitchell/
www.facebook.com/ProphetessNalo?mibextid=2JQ9oc
www.newvictoriesint
www.ernational.com/
https://www.twitter.com/MitchellNalo

# Coaches Empower Individuals to Maximize Their Potential

*By Nalo Thomas Mitchell*

As we walk through this journey called life, we realize that we all have a divine destiny that is cultivated by our personal belief system, the decisions we make, and our faith. Faith is not merely about the tangible and visible aspects of life. It's also concerned with the unseen and requires that one trusts in what cannot be seen by the naked eye. This conviction impacts decisions made by individuals as they search for the right life coach.

Coaching, as defined by Webster's Dictionary, is "the act of training intensively through instruction and demonstration." By taking the time to reflect on our own actions and behaviors, we can become better coaches to those around us and make a positive difference in their lives.

Our first life coaches are often our parents, grandparents, family members, pastors, religious leaders, and those who love us unconditionally from the moment we are born. As we journey through life, we encounter countless milestones that shape who we are as individuals. From taking our first steps to achieving academic and professional success, we owe it all to those who cheered us on along the way. It's the encouraging words and unwavering support that helped to push us past our limits and reach new heights. Whether it was singing in a play, performing at a piano recital, or earning a postgraduate degree, these achievements would not be possible without the support of our loved ones.

Family often extends beyond bloodlines. Family friends (those who do not share our DNA) can also play a significant and vital role in our lives. They can cheer us on to believe in ourselves beyond our natural human capabilities and thought processes.

While growing up in the Midwest, I was fortunate enough to

have several life coaches before the title even existed. My mother, Deidre, was an amazing and successful educator who served Chicago Public Schools for more than thirty years as an athletic director, track coach, PE teacher, dance teacher, and ultimately, a life coach. She was instrumental in helping many young people obtain college scholarships—in some cases, full rides—to attend universities throughout the United States. Many of her former students continued their careers in dance and music and launched their very own dance studios and businesses.

Growing up in the arts as my mom danced and performed for a modern dance company is one of many fond memories that I have of my childhood. The women in the company, who were of various cultural backgrounds, all served as a mentor to me. But my mom was my life coach, and performing and teaching were some of her life's passions!

As the woman stood before the crowd and the curtain opened at the inaugural performance, she stood there thinking about the count of every dancer—"One, two, three, four, five, six, seven, eight."

And the lights bloomed upon her beautiful honeysuckle face that resembled a star who was born for greatness. She dazzled the crowd with her Jazz moves, plié, relevé, and sashay across the stage at Mundelein College, Navy Pier, Kennedy College, and Chicago's Auditorium Theater. There she stood with confidence and boldness with the steps of an accomplished dancer as her daughter watched and beamed with pride, thinking, "That's my mom!"

The woman would rein in the crowd with her modern and ballet dance moves that were relevant to the time and beat of the music and African drums. She and her accompaniments in the performance would honor The Lord through spiritual dance and rhythmic songs. The jazz/soul duo ensemble that honored the Queen of Soul herself, the late Ms. Aretha Franklin, would have the audience coming alive.

The modern dances that spoke of the complexities of heartache, pain, tragedy, and triumph were a testament to life itself. But, in the audience was the woman's precious daughter who admired her momma, her first life coach.

My grandmothers, aunts and uncles were my first life coaches as well. They loved and cherished me and taught me so much about the importance of putting God first, goal-setting and the importance of having a career and pension. They would correct me out of love when I made mistakes because they wanted the best for me. Their love was integral in allowing me to see God's amazing grace in the lives of His people, and I am forever thankful for each of them.

Life coaches desire to see individuals level up in life and obtain their personal life goals. They help individuals navigate challenging situations through instruction, direction, encouragement, and constructive criticism. Their empathy and support help guide individuals through important life decisions to reach their next dimension and full potential in life.

As phenomenal women leaders and life coaches, we must ask ourselves the tough questions that enable us to grow in our roles. Are we living up to our full potential as coaches? Do we demonstrate authenticity, productivity, and positivity in our daily lives so other women can reach their full capabilities? When we miss the mark (as we all do sometimes), are we vulnerable enough with our accountability partner to admit our mistakes and work through them? Or do we just sweep them under the rug, hoping things will change without effort and honesty? To be better coaches, we must start by being honest about where **we** are in life.

Accountability is vital in today's world, when so many women (and people) are struggling with their inner-being and insurmountable life challenges. Change and progress go hand-in-hand and it doesn't happen instantaneously or overnight. It takes one step at a time—mile by mile it's a trial, yard by yard it's hard, and inch by inch it's a cinch. Move and keep going; movement brings about progress and in time, progress produces change.

Accountability begins and ends with honesty. As life coaches, we understand that we cannot pour from an empty glass. We must be accountable for our own personal growth to have the ability to help others reach their full potential. Remember, taking care of ourselves is not selfish, it's necessary. Let's continue to strive for growth and lead by example as life coaches who pour from glasses that are full.

Life coaches are more than just goal setters; they can serve as keys to someone experiencing a breakthrough in their lives. They are builders, strategy makers, movers and shakers, homemakers, CEOs, and directors. They're strategic individuals who use pieces of a puzzle to build upon a narrative to help others achieve their dreams and goals. It's like building a house—there are steps that are built upon piece by piece. There's an architect and contractor/builder, who all know that the ground must be dug up before the foundation can be laid, which must be done before the home can be built. This is how it is with goal setting. Some of the old habits and old ways of thinking and doing things must be dug up before the new structures form a foundation of living a life of mindfulness.

So, let's challenge ourselves to be the best coaches we can be, both for ourselves and for others. Let's strive for authenticity, excellence, productivity, and positivity in all that we do. And let's remember that admitting our mistakes and being vulnerable are not signs of weakness, but rather strengths that can lead to growth and success.

It's important to take a moment to appreciate the people in our lives who have been our biggest supporters, whether they are relatives or friends. Their love helped to build and guide us. We owe so much to our life coaches and to those who have invested their time, energy, and love into our lives.

If you have a coach in your life, take a moment to thank them today. And if you don't, consider seeking out a mentor or coach to help guide you on your journey to success.

# Thank You

We want to thank you, dear reader, for taking time to read this. If you found these stories helpful please take a moment to leave a review on Amazon.com or Goodreads.com

# Other Books

**Everyday Woman: All About You**

*By Galit Ventura-Rozen and Angela Giles*

**Everyday Woman's Guide to Doing What You Love:**

51 Stories from Purpose Driven Women

**Everyday Woman's Guide to Success in Your Business:**

27 Stories from Successful Women

**Everyday Woman's Guide to The Mindset Of A Successful Woman:** 39 Stories from Successful Women

**Everyday Woman's Guide to Living Your Best life:** 32 women Share Their Wisdom

**The Successful Woman's Mindset:** 21 Journeys to Success

Made in the USA
Coppell, TX
30 March 2024

30732892R00115